Intoduction to the Buddhist Scriptures

Nina van Gorkom

2019

Published in 2019 by:
Zolag
32 Woodnook Road
Streatham
London
SW16 6TZ
www.zolag.co.uk

ISBN 9781897633359

British Library Cataloguing in Publication Data
A CIP record for this book is available from the British Library

Contents

Preface

This book is a follow-up of my book "The Buddha's Path", where I have explained the basic principles of the Buddha's teachings. In this book I would like to introduce the reader to the Buddhist scriptures which contain the teaching of the Buddha. I will quote more extensively from the texts with the aim to encourage the reader to study the texts himself. In that way he can verify himself that the Buddha's words were directed to the practice of what he taught, in particular to the development of right understanding of all phenomena of our life. In the Appendix I have enumerated the texts of the Tipiṭaka and their commentaries with their translations into English. For the now following chapters I have used many ideas of the lectures for a radio program in Thailand by Sujin Boriharnwanaket. She quotes extensively from all three parts of the scriptures, explains their meaning and inspires people to relate them to their daily life. If we merely read the texts with the purpose of intellectual understanding, we fail to see the message they contain for our life at this moment and we do not understand the goal of the Buddha's teachings.

Chapter 1

Abhidhamma in the Scriptures

We read in the "Kindred Sayings" (Saḷāyatana Vagga, Kindred Sayings about Feeling, Book I, § 7, Sickness):

> Once the Exalted One was staying near Vesālī, in Great Grove, at the Hall of the Peaked Gable.
>
> Then the Exalted One at eventide rising from his solitude went to visit the sick-ward, and on reaching it sat down on a seat made ready. So seated the Exalted One addressed the monks, saying:—
>
> "Monks, a monk should meet his end collected and composed[1]. This is our instruction to you. And how, monks, is one collected?
>
> Herein, monks, a monk dwells, contemplating the body in the body... feeling in the feeling... consciousness in consciousness... dhamma in dhamma, ardent, composed and thoughtful, having put away in this world the dejection arising from craving. Thus, monks, is a monk collected.
>
> And how, monks, is a monk composed?

[1]Collected and composed are in this text the translation of : with sati sampajañña, with mindfulness and understanding. The four applications of mindfulness which then follow have been explained in Vol. I, Ch 8.

Herein, monks, in his going forth and in his returning a monk acts composedly. In looking in front and looking behind, he acts composedly. In bending or relaxing (his limbs) he acts composedly. In wearing his robe and bearing outer robe and bowl, in eating, drinking, chewing, and tasting he acts composedly. In easing himself, in going, standing, sitting, sleeping, waking, in speaking and keeping silence he acts composedly. Thus, monks, is a monk composed.

Monks, a monk should meet his end collected and composed. This is our instruction to you.

Now, monks, as that monk dwells collected, composed, earnest, ardent, strenuous, there arises in him feeling that is pleasant, and he thus understands: 'There is arisen in me this pleasant feeling. Now that is owing to something, not without cause. Owing to what? Owing to this same body. Now this body is impermanent, compounded, arisen owing to something. It is owing to this impermanent body, which has so arisen, that pleasant feeling has arisen as a consequence, and how can that be permanent?'

Thus he dwells contemplating impermanence in body and pleasant feeling, he dwells contemplating their transience, their waning, their ceasing, the giving of them up. As he thus dwells contemplating impermanence in body and pleasant feeling, contemplating their transience... the lurking tendency to lust for body and pleasant feeling is abandoned.

So also as regards painful feeling... the lurking tendency to repugnance for body and painful feeling is abandoned.

So also as regards neutral feeling... the lurking tendency to ignorance of body and neutral feeling is abandoned.

If he feels a pleasant feeling he understands: 'That is impermanent, I do not cling to it. It has no lure for me.' If

> he feels a painful feeling he understands likewise. So also if he feels a neutral feeling.
>
> If he feels a pleasant feeling, he feels it as released from bondage to it.
>
> So also, if he feels a painful feeling and a neutral feeling, he feels it as one released from bondage to it.
>
> When he feels a feeling that his bodily endurance has reached its limit, he knows that he so feels. When he feels a feeling that life has reached its limit, he knows that he so feels. He understands: When body breaks up, after life is used up, all my experiences in this world will lose their lure and grow cold.
>
> Just as, monks, because of oil and because of a wick a lamp keeps burning, but, when oil and wick are used up, the lamp would go out because it is not fed. Even so, monks, a monk, when he feels a feeling that his bodily endurance has reached its limit, that his life has reached its limit, when he feels a feeling that, when body breaks up, after life is used up, all his experience in this world will lose its lure and grow cold,- he knows that he so feels."

This sutta contains the essence of the Buddha's teaching: the development of satipatthāna, right understanding of mental phenomena and physical phenomena, which leads to the eradication of all defilements. Just as a lamp will go out when oil and wick are used up the person who has eradicated defilements will not be reborn.

The Buddha taught about the realities which can be directly experienced in daily life when they appear, such as seeing, hearing, feeling, hardness or sound. All these phenomena are real in the absolute or ultimate sense. Absolute or ultimate truth is different from conventional truth [2]. If one has never heard of the Buddha's teachings one only knows what is real in conventional sense. We think of ourselves and of the world around us, of people, animals, trees, and they seem to last. The world, person, animal or tree are real in conventional sense.

[2] I explained the difference in The Buddha's Path, Ch 3 and 4.

The world and everything in it can only appear because consciousness arises just for a moment, thinks about it and then falls away immediately. Consciousness, in Pāli : citta, is real in the absolute sense. The Buddha taught that in the absolute sense our life consists of mental phenomena, in Pāli: nāma, and physical phenomena, in Pāli: rūpa. Citta is nāma, it experiences an object, whereas rūpa does not experience anything. There are no mind and body which last and which belong to a self or person; what we take for our mind and body are only different nāmas and rūpas, each with their own characteristic which can be experienced one at a time when it appears. They arise because of their appropriate conditions and then fall away immediately. They are impermanent and they do not belong to a self, they have no owner. There is only one citta arising at a time, but each citta is accompanied by several mental factors, in Pāli: cetasikas. Both citta and cetasika are nāma. Some cetasikas, such as feeling and remembrance accompany each citta, whereas unwholesome qualities such as attachment and aversion accompany only unwholesome cittas and wholesome qualities such as kindnes, generosity or understanding accompany wholesome cittas. Citta cannot arise without cetasikas and cetasikas cannot arise without citta, they condition one another. They arise together, experience the same object and then fall away together. Thus, what we call "person" is actually citta, cetasika and rūpa which arise and fall away. Citta, cetasika and rūpa are the three paramattha dhammas which are conditioned: they arise because of conditions and then fall away. There is a fourth paramattha dhamma which is unconditioned, which does not arise and fall away and this is nibbāna. Nibbāna is the reality which can only be experienced at the moment enlightenment is attained.

The development of right understanding of what is real in the ultimate sense is the only way leading to the eradication of defilements. When we study the scriptures, no matter whether it is the Vinaya, the Book of Discipline for the monks, the Suttanta or Discourses, or the Abhidhamma, we should never forget this goal. The Vinaya contains rules and guidelines for the monk's behaviour which can help him to reach perfection, the state of the arahat, who has eradicated all defilements. The Suttanta or Suttas are discourses of the Buddha to people of different levels of understanding at different places. In these discourses the Buddha speaks about birth, old age, sickness and death. He speaks about the suffering in the world and the cause of all suffering which is craving. He explains what is unwholesome and what is wholesome or beneficial, he points out the danger of defilements and the way to eradicate them by the development of understanding of all that is real. The Abhidhamma contains the description of all mental phenomena and physical phenomena of our life, their different conditioning factors and the way they are related to each other.

In the Abhidhamma all paramattha dhammas, ultimate realities, are enumerated and classified in detail, but also in the Suttas the Buddha explained about paramattha dhammas, about nāma and rūpa, in order to help people to gain understanding. The Suttas are mostly, but not entirely, in terms of conventional language. The Buddha knew the different accumulated inclinations of people and thus he chose the wording best suited to the persons addressed. He spoke to monks, laypeople, brahmins and philosophers who adhered to other beliefs. He made use of parables or of examples of events in daily life in order to help people to understand paramattha dhammas. Right understanding of paramattha dhammas should be developed in order to eliminate wrong view of realities. The study of the Abhidhamma helps us to have more understanding of what the Buddha taught in the suttas.

Not all people were ready to grasp what paramattha dhammas are, and therefore the Buddha would give them a "gradual discourse", or a discourse "in due order". We read, for example in the "Verses of Uplift" (Khuddaka Nikāya, Minor Anthologies), Ch V, 3, that, when the Buddha was staying near Rājagaha, in Bamboo Grove, a leper, named Suppabuddha, saw from afar that the Buddha was teaching dhamma to a great many people. He wanted to draw near the crowd, hoping to obtain some food. He noticed that there was no alms-giving, but that the Buddha was teaching dhamma and then he decided to listen. We read:

> Now the Exalted One, grasping with his mind the thoughts of all that assembly, said to himself: Who, I wonder, of

> those present is of growth to understand dhamma? And the Exalted One saw Suppabuddha, the leper, sitting in that assembly, and at the sight he thought: This one here is of growth to understand dhamma. So for the sake of Suppabuddha, the leper, he gave a talk dealing in due order with these topics: on almsgiving, virtue, the heaven world, of the danger, meanness and corruption of sense-desires, and the profit of getting free of them.
>
> And when the Exalted One knew that the heart of Suppabuddha, the leper, was ready, softened, unbiassed, elated and believing, then he unfolded those dhamma-teachings which the awakened ones have themselves discovered, namely: Dukkha, arising, ending, the Way.
>
> Then just as a white cloth, free from stains, is ready to receive the dye, even so in Suppabuddha, the leper, as he sat there in that very seat, arose the pure, stainless dhamma-sight, the knowledge that whatsoever is of a nature to arise, that also is of a nature to end. And Suppabuddha, the leper, saw dhamma, reached dhamma, understood dhamma, plunged into dhamma, crossed beyond doubting, was free from all questionings, won confidence, and needing none other in the Master's message [3], rose from his seat, advanced to the Exalted One and sat down at one side...

Suppabuddha listened to the Buddha's exposition of the four noble Truths: dukkha, the cause of dukkha, the cessation of dukkha and the way leading to the cessation of dukkha which is the eightfold Path [4]. While Suppabuddha listened he attained the first stage of enlightenment, the stage of the sotāpanna. He could not have attained enlightenment if he had not known what dhammas, realities, are. While he was seeing and hearing he had to be aware of the nāmas

[3] He had personal conviction of the truth. The sotāpanna has eradicated doubt about realities and he has an unshakable confidence in the Triple Gem.

[4] As I explained in The Buddha'a Path, Ch 1 and 2, realities which are impermanent are unsatisfactory, dukkha.

and rūpas which were appearing and he had to penetrate their true nature. He could attain enlightenment because he had accumulated wisdom also in past lives.

We cannot understand the deep meaning of the suttas if we have no basic understanding of the paramattha dhammas as they have been described in the Abhidhamma. We cannot understand what has been stated in this sutta about Suppabuddha's enlightenment if we do not know that citta, cetasika and rūpa, thus, paramattha dhammas, are the objects of insight. Suppabuddha had to clearly know the difference between the characteristics of nāma and rūpa as they appeared one at a time, and he had to realize them as conditioned realities before he could penetrate their impermanence, their nature of dukkha and of non-self [5]. It takes an endlessly long time, even many lives, to develop understanding. However, a moment of understanding is never lost, it is accumulated. In the Seventh Book of the Abhidhamma, the "Paṭṭhāna", translated as "Conditional Relations", different types of conditions for realities have been taught. One of these is the contiguity-condition (anantara-paccaya): each citta which arises is a condition for the succeeding one by way of contiguity-condition. Defilements and good qualities which arose in the past, even in past lives, are accumulated from one moment of citta to the next one, since each citta conditions the following one by way of contiguity-condition. The Abhidhamma clarifies how we accumulate different inclinations and how they condition the cittas arising at the present time.

We read further on that Suppabuddha went away after having heard the discourse and was then killed by a calf. When the monks asked the Buddha about Suppabuddha's rebirth the Buddha explained that he was a sotāpanna, bound for full enlightenment. A sotāpanna cannot be reborn in an unhappy plane. The monks then asked why he was born as a poor, wretched leper. The Buddha answered that in a former life he had insulted a "Silent Buddha". Because of that deed he was reborn in hell and in his last life he was born as a leper. In that life he became a sotāpanna and then he was reborn in a heavenly plane.

[5] As I explained in Vol. I, Ch 7, insight is developed in different stages.

We read in this sutta about kamma which produces result, but it is a subject which is difficult to understand. The study of the Abhidhamma is most helpful to gain more understanding of the different conditions for the nāmas and rūpas of our life, including the condition of kamma which produces vipāka. We have read in the above-quoted sutta about the result Suppabuddha received when a calf caused his death. Not only pain felt at an accident is vipāka, but also seeing, hearing and the other sense-impressions are vipāka. They are vipākacittas arising time and again in daily life. The Abhidhamma teaches in detail about all the different types of kusala cittas, of akusala cittas and of cittas which are neither kusala nor akusala, including vipākacittas, and about all the different cetasikas which accompany cittas. We learn about the different objects cittas experience through the senses and the mind-door, and about the defilements arising on account of what is experienced. Also in the suttas we read about the experience of objects through the senses and the defilements which arise, but without the study of the Abhidhamma we cannot fully understand the sutta texts. I will illustrate this with a quotation from another sutta. We read in the "Kindred Sayings" (IV, Saḷāyatana Vagga, Kindred Sayings on Sense, Second Fifty, Ch 5, § 98, Restraint) that the Buddha said to the monks:

> I will teach you, monks, restraint and lack of restraint. Do you listen to it. And how, monks, is one unrestrained?
>
> There are, monks, objects cognizable by the eye, objects desirable, pleasant, delightful and dear, passion-fraught, inciting to lust. If a monk be enamoured of them, if he welcome them, if he persist in clinging to them, thus should he understand: "I am falling back in profitable states. This was called 'falling back' by the Exalted One."
>
> (the same is said with regard to the other sense-doors and the mind-door.)
>
> And how, monks, is one restrained?
>
> There are objects cognizable by the eye... If a monk be not enamoured of them, if he welcome them not, ... thus

> should he understand: "I am not falling back in profitable states. This was called 'not falling back' by the Exalted One." Thus, monks, is one restrained.

The Abhidhamma helps us to understand the different functions of cittas arising in a process of cittas which experience objects through the six doors. In a process of cittas which experience an object through one of the sense-doors there are moments of vipāka and there are kusala cittas or akusala cittas which arise on account of the object which is experienced. The cittas arising in such a process arise each because of their own conditions and in a fixed order; there is no self who can direct the arising of particular cittas. There is no self who is unrestrained or restrained. When we read about the monk who is enamoured of the objects experienced through eyes, ears, or through the other senses, we may not realize that we all have attachment time and again after seeing, hearing and the other sense-impressions. When we read the above-quoted sutta with understanding of different cittas arising in processes we will see that this sutta reminds us of our defilements arising in daily life, even at this moment. If we do not know that defilements and wholesome qualities are cetasikas, conditioned realities, we may take them for self. We may cling to a concept of self who is practising the eightfold Path, whereas in reality wholesome cetasikas are performing their functions. We read in the suttas about the exertion of energy or effort for what is wholesome and about right effort of the eightfold Path. If we do not know that effort is a cetasika which can arise with akusala citta as well as with kusala citta there are bound to be many misunderstandings concerning the development of kusala and in particular the development of the eightfold Path. We read, for example, in the "Gradual Sayings" (II, Book of the Fours, Ch II, § 3, Effort)[6]:

> There are four right efforts, O monks. What four?
>
> Herein, a monk rouses his will not to permit the arising of evil, unwholesome states that have not arisen- to abandon

[6]I am using the translation of Ven. Nyanaponika, in Anguttara Nikāya, An Anthology I, Wheel no. 155-158, Kandy.

> evil, unwholesome states already arisen- to arouse wholesome states that have not yet arisen- to maintain wholesome states already arisen and not allow them to disappear; he makes an effort (for it), stirs up his energy, exerts his mind and strives.

Someone may believe that whenever he tries to develop the eightfold Path there is right effort which is wholesome, but in reality there may be effort arising with akusala citta rooted in attachment, he may take effort for "my effort". Mindfulness arises because of its appropriate conditions, not by trying to make it arise. When awareness and right understanding of nāma and rūpa arise there is at that moment also right effort which accompanies the kusala citta. Thus, it is essential to study details of cetasikas which accompany the different types of citta. The study of the Abhidhamma can help us to have a more precise understanding of the realities of daily life.

Some people doubt whether the Abhidhamma is the Buddha's teaching. The commentator Buddhaghosa explains[7] that the Buddha, at the attainment of enlightenment, penetrated the truth of all realities, and that he in the fourth week after his enlightenment contemplated the contents of the seven books of the Abhidhamma. He preached the Abhidhamma first to the devas of the heavenly plane of the "Thirtythree", headed by his mother. After that he conveyed the method of the Abhidhamma to Sāriputta.

Thus, the codified Abhidhamma literature as we have it today goes back to the Buddha's chief disciple Sāriputta. When we study the Abhidhamma and the suttas and compare them, we will notice that also numerous suttas are in terms of paramattha dhammas, dealing with the khandhas (aggregates), the elements, the sense-fields (āyatanas) and the cittas. Also the Vinaya deals with cittas and with many different degrees of defilements which can accompany citta. The Vinaya reminds the monk to scrutinize himself, to be aware also of akusala cittas. While the monk goes out to collect almsfood and while he accomplishes his daily tasks he should develop mindfulness and un-

---

[7]In the "Expositor I, Introductory Discourse. See further on in this chapter about the person of Buddhaghosa.

derstanding of nāma and rūpa. All three parts of the Buddhist scriptures are in conformity with each other, they help people to develop right understanding of all realities, each in their own situation of life. Historical reasons may not cure doubts about the authenticity of the scriptures, but careful examination and consideration of the contents of the Buddhist teachings themselves can convince us of their authenticity and their immense value for the development of the way leading to freedom from all suffering.

When someone takes up the first book of the Abidhamma, the "Dhammasangaṇi", translated as "a Buddhist Manual of Psychological Ethics", he may feel confused about the many classifications and enumerations of cittas, of their accompanying cetasikas and of rūpas. These are not abstract categories just to be read and memorized, but they are realities which arise time and again in daily life. When they appear they can be objects of awareness and right understanding. The development of satipatthāna, right understanding of nāma and rūpa as impermanent, dukkha and non-self, is the aim of the teaching of the Abhidhamma. The first book of the Abhidhamma should be read together with its commentary the "Atthasālinī", translated in two volumes as "The Expositor". The great commentator Buddhaghosa, who lived in the sixth century A.D., wrote this commentary. The footnotes of the translation of the first book of the Abhidhamma refer to the corresponding parts in its commentary, and the reader will see for himself that the commentary is most helpful for the correct understanding of the Abhidhamma[8]. Buddhaghosa came from India to Sri Lanka where he edited and rendered into the Pāli language ancient Singhalese commentaries he found there. The commentaries to most of the Buddhist scriptures are from his hand, but they are based on the ancient commentaries. The "Visuddhimagga", an encyclopedia of the teachings written by Buddhaghosa, which is translated as "The Path of Purification", and also the "Abhidhammattha Sangaha", a compendium of the Abhidhamma written by Anuruddha [9], are of great assistance for

---

[8]In my "Abhidhamma in Daily Life" I tried to give an introduction to the study of the Abhidhamma.

[9]The time this was written is not sure, but it must have been between the 8th and 12th century A.D. This has been translated as "A Manual of Abhidhamma" by

the understanding of the Abhidhamma.

In the above-quoted sutta on restraint and lack of restraint we read that the monk who is not enticed by pleasant objects is restrained. Someone may have restraint by temporarily suppressing his likes and dislikes, but when there are conditions for defilements they will arise again. Only through the development of right understanding of realities can there be restraint which is enduring. The development of satipatthāna is exclusively the teaching of the Buddha and thus this is implied in all parts of the scriptures, also when it is not expressively mentioned. We read in the "Middle Length Sayings" (II, 97, Discourse with Dhānañjāni) that Sāriputta taught the brahman Dhānañjāni when he was sick about the meditations which are the "Divine Abidings" of lovingkindness, compassion, sympathetic joy and equanimity. With these meditations, when they are developed, jhāna or absorption can be attained. However, jhāna is not the goal of the Buddha's teachings. We read that the Buddha said to Sāriputta:

> "But why did you, Sāriputta, although there was something further to be done, having established the brahman Dhānañjāni (only) in the less, in the Brahma-world, rising from your seat, depart?"
>
> "It occurred to me, Lord: 'These brahmans are very intent on the Brahma-world. Suppose I were to show the brahman Dhānañjāni the way to companionship with Brahmā?"'
>
> "Sāriputta, the brahman Dhānañjāni has died and has uprisen in the Brahma-world."

This sutta reminds us not to forget the goal of the Buddha's teachings, that is: the eradication of defilements through the development of satipatthāna. We cannot understand any sutta if we do not begin to develop understanding of the nāma or rūpa which appears in our daily life. In the following sutta the importance is stressed of listening to the teachings, considering them and putting them into practice. We read in the "Kindred Sayings"(II, Nidāna-vagga, Ch XX, Kindred

---

Ven. Nārada, Colombo, and as "Compendium of Philosophy" in a P.T.S. edition.

Sayings on Parables, § 7, The Drum-peg) that the Buddha said to the monks:

> Once upon a time, monks, the Dasārahas had a kettle-drum called Summoner. As it began to split the Dasārahas fixed in ever another peg, until the time came that the Summoner's original drumhead had vanished and only the framework of pegs remained.
>
> Even so, monks, will the monks become in the future. Those Suttantas uttered by the Tathāgata, deep, deep in meaning, not of the world, dealing with the void, to these when uttered, they will not listen, they will not lend a ready ear, they will not bring to them an understanding heart, they will not deem those doctrines that which should be learnt by heart, that which should be mastered.
>
> But those Suttantas which are made by poets, which are poetry, which are a manifold of words, a manifold of phrases, alien, the utterances of disciples, to these when uttered they will listen, they will lend a ready ear, they will bring an understanding heart, they will deem these doctrines that which should be learnt by heart, which should be mastered. Thus it is, monks, that the Suttantas uttered by the Tathāgata, deep, deep in meaning, not of the world, dealing with the void, will disappear.
>
> Wherefore, monks, you are thus to train yourselves:— To these very Suttantas will we listen, will we give a ready ear, to these will we bring an understanding heart. And we will deem these doctrines that which should be learnt by heart, and mastered:— even thus.

The Buddha's teachings will disappear by wrong understanding of them and by wrong practice. Today we are fortunate that we still have access to the teachings. Therefore, we should not neglect to study them and to put them into practice.

Chapter 2

The Long Road

The Buddha had at his enlightenment penetrated the four noble Truths. He had become a Fully Enlightened One who could teach the truth to others and show them the Path leading to the eradication of defilements. In the scriptures we read about countless monks, nuns and laypeople, who listened to the Buddha and also penetrated the four noble Truths. They could do so because they had already during innumerable lives accumulated right understanding of all realities appearing through the six doors. We read time and again in the scriptures that the Buddha explained about the objects which are experienced through eyes, ears, nose, tongue, body and mind. We read, for example, in the "Kindred Sayings" (V, Mahā-vagga, Book XII, Kindred Sayings about the Truths, Ch II, 4, Sphere of Sense) that the Buddha said:

> Monks, there are these four ariyan truths. What four? The ariyan truth about dukkha, that about the arising of dukkha, that about the ceasing of dukkha, and the ariyan truth about the practice that leads to the ceasing of dukkha.
>
> And what, monks, is the ariyan truth about dukkha?
>
> Dukkha, it should be said, is the six personal spheres of sense. What six?

> The sense-sphere of the eye, of the ear, the nose, the tongue, the body, the mind. This, monks, is called "the ariyan truth about dukkha."
>
> And what, monks, is the ariyan truth about the arising of dukkha?
>
> It is that craving that leads back to rebirth, along with the lure and the lust that linger longingly now here, now there: namely, the craving for sensual delight, the craving to be born again, the craving for existence to end. This is the ariyan truth about the arising of dukkha.
>
> And what, monks, is the ariyan truth about the ceasing of dukkha?
>
> Verily it is the utter passionless cessation of, the giving up, the forsaking, the release from, the absence of longing for this craving. This is the ariyan truth about the ceasing of dukkha.
>
> And what, monks, is the ariyan truth about the practice that leads to the ceasing of dukkha?
>
> Verily it is this ariyan eightfold way, to wit: right view, right thinking, right speech, right action, right livelihood, right effort, right mindfulness, right concentration. This is the ariyan truth about the practice that leads to the ceasing of dukkha.
>
> These, monks, are the four ariyan truths. Wherefore, an effort must be made to realize: This is dukkha. This is the arising of dukkha. This is the ceasing of dukkha. This is the practice that leads to the ceasing of dukkha.

"Sphere of sense" is the translation of the Pāli term "āyatana". We read in the "Book of Analysis" (Vibhanga), the second book of the Abhidhamma [1], in Chapter 3, "Analysis of the Bases", about the

---

[1] This book can be read together with its commentary, the "Sammohavinodani", attributed to Buddhaghosa and translated as "The Dispeller of Delusion", in two volumes. The commentary is most helpful for the understanding of the Abhid-

twelve āyatanas, here translated as "bases". They are: the eye, the ear, the nose, the tongue, the body, the mind, visible object, sound, odour, flavour, tangible object and mind-object. The āyatana of the mind includes all cittas. Thus, nāma and rūpa can be classified in several ways and the classification by way of āyatanas is one of them. In this section of the "Book of Analysis", in § 1, "Analysis according to the Discourses", it is said of each of the bases that it is "impermanent, dukkha, non-self, a changeable thing". This is a reminder that the āyatanas are objects of insight, otherwise their true nature cannot be penetrated. Here we see again that the Abhidhamma points to the goal, the development of right understanding.

Some people find it monotonous that in the scriptures it has been stressed again and again that the realities appearing through the six doors should be understood. There are no other realities besides those which appear one at a time through the sense-doors and the mind-door. The Buddha repeatedly spoke about those realities for fortyfive years so that people would begin to be mindful of them. We know that seeing is different from hearing, but when they actually appear we are ignorant of them. Citta arises and falls away very quickly; it seems that seeing and hearing occur at the same time, but in reality this is impossible. There can only be one citta at a time which experiences one object. The Buddha taught again and again about the realities appearing through the six doors in order to remind us of them; we are most of the time forgetful of them when they appear. We are absorbed in thinking of what we saw or heard, of concepts which are not real in the absolute sense, instead of developing understanding of absolute realities such as seeing, hearing or thinking.

We read in the above-quoted sutta about craving which is the second noble Truth. Craving for all the objects we experience arises time and again because it has been accumulated. We are not only attached to visible object, sound and the other sense-objects we experience, but also to seeing, hearing and the experiences through the other doors. We read in the sutta about a threefold craving: craving

---

hamma, that is, the understanding of one's own life. Buddhaghosa illustrates the meaning of the realities taught in the "Book of Analysis" in a lively way with examples from daily life.

for sensual delight (kāma-tanhā), for becoming (bhava-tanhā) and for non-becoming (vibhava-taṇhā)[2]. Even when someone is not attached to sense-pleasures he may be attached to jhāna or absorption concentration and rebirth in higher planes of existence which is the result of jhāna. Then there is craving for becoming. This kind of craving may be without wrong view or with wrong view. When it is accompanied by wrong view it is clinging to eternity-belief, the belief in the existence of a persisting personality. The craving for non-becoming is always accompanied by wrong view, it is clinging to annihilation, the belief that there is annihilation at death.

So long as there is any form of clinging there are conditions for the continuation of the cycle of birth and death and thus there will be dukkha. The sutta exhorts us to develop the eightfold Path since this leads to the end of dukkha. Before the truth of dukkha can be realized right understanding of nāma and rūpa has to be developed stage by stage, and this is an endlessly long process. Also the Buddha had to accumulate understanding very gradually during his lives as a Bodhisatta before he could realize the four noble Truths. We read in the "Gradual Sayings" (I, Book of the Threes, Ch XI, Enlightenment, § 101, Before) that the Buddha said:

> Before my enlightenment, monks, when I was yet but a Bodhisat, this occurred to me: What, I wonder, is the satisfaction in the world, what is the misery in the world, what is the escape therefrom?
>
> Then, monks, this occurred to me: That condition in the world owing to which pleasure arises, owing to which arises happiness,— that is the satisfaction in the world. That impermanence, that suffering, that changeability in the world,— that is the misery in the world. That restraint, that riddance of desire and passion in the world,— that is the escape therefrom.
>
> So long, monks, as I did not thoroughly comprehend, as it really is, the satisfaction in the world as such, the misery in

[2]These three are often mentioned in the scriptures. See also, for example, the "Book of Analysis", Ch 4, § 2, the Truth of the Cause.

> the world as such, the escape therefrom as such, so long did I not discern the meaning of being enlightened with perfect enlightenment unsurpassed in the world with it devas, its Māras and Brahmās, together with the host of recluses and brāhmins, of devas and mankind. But, monks, when I fully comprehended, as it really is, the satisfaction in the world as such, the misery in the world as such, the escape therefrom as such,- then did I discern the meaning of being enlightened in the world... Then did knowledge and insight arise in me, thus: Sure is my heart's release. This is my last birth. Now is there no more becoming again.
>
> Seeking satisfaction in the world, monks, I had pursued my way. That satisfaction in the world I found. In so far as satisfaction existed in the world, by insight I saw it well. Seeking for the misery in the world, monks, I had pursued my way. That misery in the world I found. In so far as misery existed in the world, by insight I saw it well. Seeking for the escape from the world, monks, I had pursued my way. That escape from the world I found. In so far as escape from the world existed, by insight I saw it well...

With regard to the words, "Seeking satisfaction in the world, monks, I had pursued my way", the commentary to this sutta (the Manorathapūranī) states: "Ever since the time when he was the brāhmin Sumedha." Aeons and aeons ago the Buddha was born as the brahmin prince Sumedha. During that life he made the resolve to become a Buddha in the future. We read in the above quoted sutta, "That satisfaction in the world I found. In so far as satisfaction existed in the world, by insight I saw it well." The Buddha had to develop as a Bodhisatta right understanding of all realities, also of his defilements. He did not avoid being aware of sense-pleasures.

We read in the "Chronicle of the Buddhas"(II A, Account of Sumedha, Khuddaka Nikāya, Buddhavamsa, translated in "The Minor Anthologies of the Pāli Canon, Part III) that Sumedha who lived in great luxury, decided to retire from worldly life in order to seek the way to the end of the cycle of birth and death. We read (vs. 7- 10):

> Sitting in seclusion I thought thus then: "Again-becoming is dukkha, also the breaking up of the physical frame.
>
> Liable to birth, liable to ageing, liable to disease am I then; I will seek the peace that is unageing, undying, secure.
>
> Suppose I, casting aside this putrid body filled with various ordures, should go indifferent, unconcerned?
>
> There is, there must be that Way; it is impossible for it not to be. I shall seek that Way for the utter release from becoming...

When he saw people clearing a way for the Buddha Dīpaṅkara he also helped clearing a section of the road. We read (vs. 52-57):

> Loosening my hair, spreading my bark-garments and piece of hide there in the mire, I lay down prone.
>
> "Let the Buddha go treading on me with his disciples. Do not let him tread in the mire- it will be for my welfare."
>
> While I was lying on the earth it was thus in my mind: If I so wished I could burn up my defilements today.
>
> What is the use while I (remain) unknown of realizing dhamma here? Having reached omniscience, I will become a Buddha in the world with the devas.
>
> What is the use of my crossing over alone, being a man aware of my strength? Having reached omniscience, I will cause the world together with the devas to cross over.
>
> By this act of merit of mine towards the supreme among men I will reach omniscience, I will cause many people to cross over.

> Cutting through the stream of saṁsāra[3], shattering the three becomings[4], embarking in the ship of Dhamma[5], I will cause the world with the devas to cross over...

The Buddha Dīpaṇkara declared Sumedha to be a future Buddha. Sumedha reflected on the ten perfections [6] he had to accumulate from life to life. He renewed his resolution to become a Buddha many times during the lives he met other Buddhas who came after the Buddha Dīpaṇkara. He had to listen to the Dhamma preached by them, he had to consider carefully what he heard and he had to be aware of nāma and rūpa over and over again.

When we read about the Bodhisatta who had to accumulate right understanding from life to life, we can be reminded that we cannot expect to realize the four noble Truths within a short time. It is difficult to penetrate the truth that all conditioned nāmas and rūpas are arising and falling away and that they are thus dukkha. Just a moment ago sound impinged on the earsense, but it is already gone. Seeing, hearing, hardness appear, but they disappear immediately. Thinking about impermanence of realities is not the same as realizing their arising and falling away as they appear one at a time. Before paññā reaches the stage of insight which is the direct experience of the arising and falling away of nāma and rūpa, their different characteristics have to be distinguished. There must be awareness of rūpa which appears as rūpa, and awareness of nāma which appears as nāma. So long as one confuses their different characteristics one will keep on taking them for self.

In the "Discourse on the Sixfold Cleansing" (Middle Length Sayings III, 112) the Buddha speaks about a monk who declares "profound knowledge", who states that he has reached the end of birth, thus, that he is an arahat. The Buddha said that he might be questioned about his understanding so that one knows whether he speaks the truth. In this sutta we read about all realities appearing through

---

[3]The cycle of birth and death.

[4]In the sensuous planes of existence, the fine-material planes of existence (result of rūpa-jhānas) and the immaterial planes of existence (result of arūpa-jhānas).

[5]The eightfold Path.

[6]See The Buddha's Path, I, Ch 8.

the six doors which are the objects of right understanding, no matter whether someone is a beginner on the Path or an arahat.

We read that the Buddha said to the monks that one may ask the monk who states that he is an arahat the following question:

> Your reverence, these four modes of statement have been rightly pointed out by that Lord who knows and sees, perfected one, fully Self-Awakened One. What four? That which when seen is spoken of as seen, that which when heard is spoken of as heard, that which when sensed is spoken of as sensed, that which when cognised is spoken of as cognised.[7]

The Buddha said that the monk might be questioned as to what he knows and sees in respect to these "four modes of statement", so that he can say that he is freed from the "cankers" with no grasping remaining. We read that that monk would be in accordance with Dhamma were he to say:

> "I, your reverences, not feeling attracted to things seen... heard... sensed... cognised, not feeling repelled by them, independent, not infatuated, freed, released, dwell with a mind that is unconfined. So, your reverences, as I know thus, see thus in respect of these four modes of statement, I can say that my mind is freed from the cankers with no grasping (remaining)."

The Buddha said that the monks should rejoice in that monk's words and approve of them. Then a further question might be asked and this concerns his knowledge of the five khandhas or aggregates,

[7]As to the term "sensed", in Pāli: mutam, we read in the "Dhammasangaṇi"(Book II, Ch IV, § 961) that odour, taste and tangible object are rūpas which are "sensed". As to the term "cognized", this means: known through the mind-door. By way of the "four modes of statement" it is explained that all realities have to be known as they are. Seeing and the object which is seen, hearing and the object which is heard, all realities have to be clearly understood.

here referred to as the "groups of grasping"[8]. We read that that monk would be in accordance with Dhamma were he to say:

> "I, your reverences, having known that material shape (rūpa)... feeling... perception(saññā) ... the habitual tendencies (sankhārakkhandha, all cetasikas other than feeling and perception) ... consciousness, is of little strength, fading away, comfortless; by the destruction, fading away, stopping, giving up and casting out of grasping after and hankering after material shape... feeling... perception... the habitual tendencies... consciousness which are mental dogmas, biases and tendencies, I comprehend that my mind is freed..."

We then read that the person who declares himself to be an arahat might be questioned about the six elements of extension (or solidity), cohesion, radiation (temperature, appearing as heat or cold), motion[9], space[10] and consciousness[11]. Further on we read that the monk who declares himself to be an arahat might be questioned about his understanding of the twelve āyatanas, sense-fields. After that we read that he might be questioned about the tendency to pride. Pride or conceit is eradicated at the attainment of the fourth stage of enlightenment, the stage of the arahat. It cannot be eradicated at the attainment of the first three stages of enlightenment.

We then read about the monk's life of non-violence and fewness of wishes, and of his observance of purity of sīla, his moral conduct in speech and deeds. We read about his "guarding of the six doors" through mindfulness:

---

[8]As explained in Vol. I, Ch 2, all conditioned nāmas and rūpas have been classified as five khandhas.

[9]These are the four "principle rūpas" or "Great Elements". Three of them can be experienced by touch, namely, solidity, heat and motion. Cohesion cannot be experienced by touch. Rūpas do not arise singly, they arise in groups of different compositions. Each group consists of the four principle rūpas and in addition several other rūpas.

[10]The rūpa which is space, in Pāli: ākāsa, separates the different groups of rūpas from each other.

[11]Including all cittas. Apart from the classification of realities by way of six elements there are other ways of classifying realities as elements.

> If I saw visible object with the eye I was not entranced by the general appearance, I was not entranced by the detail. If I dwelt with this organ of sight uncontrolled, covetousness and dejection, evil unskilled states, might flow in. So I fared along controlling it, I guarded the organ of sight, I achieved control over it...

The same is said with regard to the other doorways. There is no self who can control the sense-doors, but at the moment of awareness there is no akusala citta on account of the objects presenting themselves. Further on we read about the monk's mindfulness in any situation, no matter what he is doing or what his posture is: walking, standing, sitting or lying down. We read, "I was one who comported myself properly", and this refers to mindfulness and right understanding of realities which appear. We then read about his attainment of the "four meditations", namely the four stages of rūpa- jhāna, fine-material absorption. Only the person who has accumulations for the attainment of jhāna can attain it, but he should not take his attainment for self, he should not cling to jhāna. The attainment of jhāna is not a necessary condition for the development of vipassanā and enlightenment. Further on we read that the monk said:

> "Thus with the mind composed, quite purified, quite clarified, without blemish, without defilement, grown soft and workable, stable, immovable, I directed my mind to the knowledge of the destruction of the cankers. I understood as it really is: This is dukkha... this the arising of dukkha... this the stopping of dukkha... this the course leading to the stopping of dukkha. I understood as it really is: These are the cankers... this is the arising of the cankers... this the stopping of the cankers... this the course leading to the stopping of the cankers. When I knew and saw this thus, my mind was freed from the canker of the sense-pleasures and my mind was freed from the canker of becoming and my mind was freed from the canker of ignorance. In freedom the knowledge came to be that I was freed and I comprehended: Destroyed is birth, brought to

> a close the Brahma-faring, done is what was to be done, there is no more of being such or so. So, your reverences, as I know thus, see thus, in respect of this consciousness-informed body and all external phenomena, I can say that my tendency to pride that 'I am the doer, mine is the doer' has been properly extirpated"....

This sutta reminds us of the conditions which are necessary for the attainment of enlightenment. The objects of which right understanding is to be developed are so near: the five khandhas, the "sense-fields" or āyatanas, the elements, all the objects which impinge time and again on the six doors, but we have accumulated such an amount of ignorance. It is a long road, but even a short moment of awareness and understanding are worth while because then there are conditions for having less ignorance.

We read in the above-quoted sutta that the monk, when he saw visible object, was not entranced by the general appearance nor by the detail. Seeing is a reality different from paying attention to the general appearance and the details of something. After seeing has fallen away we think of concepts of people and things. Concepts are not real in the ultimate sense and thus they are not objects of which right understanding is to be developed, but thinking is real and thus there can be awareness of it. We should not try to be aware only of seeing and avoid being aware of thinking, be it thinking with kusala citta or with akusala citta. We read in the "Theragāthā" (Psalms of the Brothers of the Khuddaka Nikāya), in Canto IV, 186, about the "Elder" Nāgasamāla who developed mindfulness and right understanding naturally, also when he was walking for almsfood. On his way he noticed a girl who was dancing. We read:

> Bedecked with trinkets and with pretty frock,
> Wreathed with flowers, raddled with sandal wood,
> In the main street, before the multitude
> A nautch girl danced to music's fivefold sound.
> Into the city I had gone for alms,
> And passing I beheld the dancer decked
> In brave array, like snare of Māra laid.

Thereat arose in me the deeper thought:
Attention to the fact and to the cause.
The misery of it all was manifest;
Distaste, indifference the mind possessed.
And so my heart was set at liberty.
O see the seemly order of the Dhamma!
The Threefold Wisdom[12] have I made my own,
And all the Buddha bids me do is done.

Nāgasamāla could not help noticing the girl who was dancing, but he had wise attention to all realities of his daily life, he realized them as impermanent, dukkha and non-self. He had developed all stages of insight and because of his accumulated wisdom he could attain the stage of arahatship.

We may find it difficult to be mindful when we watch on T.V. different events such as a person who is dancing or singing, or when we are engaged in conversation with other people. However, this story reminds us that we should not look for particular situations we believe to be favorable for mindfulness. Whatever situation we are in is conditioned already, and, no matter where we are, there are realities appearing through six doors: the khandhas, āyatanas or elements. In being aware of any reality which naturally appears, we take one little step on the long road to clear understanding.

[12]Namely: remembrance of former lives, the divine eye which is seeing decease and rebirth of beings according to kamma, and extinction of all defilements.

Chapter 3

Wrong View and Right View

The Buddha, after his enlightenment, preached to a group of five brāhmins a discourse about the four noble Truths. These brāhmins became his first five disciples. We read in the "Book of Discipline" (Vinaya IV, Mahāvagga, 9-14) that one of the brāhmins, Kondañña, attained the first stage of enlightenment, the stage of the sotāpanna, and that he asked for ordination under the Lord. The Buddha continued to instruct the other disciples with dhamma-talk and then also Vappa and Bhaddiya attained the first stage of enlightenment and asked for ordination. As to the two other disciples, Mahānāma and Assaji, after they received more instruction with dhamma-talk, they also attained the stage of the sotāpanna and asked for ordination. We then read that the Buddha preached another discourse to the group of five monks, the "Discourse on the Characteristic of Non-self", in which he explained that the five khandhas are non-self:

> "Body, monks, is not self. Now, were this body self, monks, this body would not tend to sickness, and one might get the chance of saying in regard to body, 'Let body become thus for me, let body not become thus for me.' But inasmuch, monks, as body is not self, therefore body tends to sickness, and one does not get the chance of saying in regard to body, 'Let body become thus for me, let body not become thus

> for me.'
>
> Feeling is not self... Perception (saññā) is not self... the 'habitual tendencies' (saṅkhārakkhandha) are not self...
>
> Consciousness is not self... Inasmuch, monks, as consciousness is not self, therefore consciousness tends to sickness, and one does not get the chance to say in regard to consciousness, 'Let consciousness become such for me, let consciousness not become thus for me.'
>
> What do you think about this, monks? Is body (rūpa) permanent or impermanent?"
>
> "Impermanent, Lord."
>
> "But is that which is impermanent painful (dukkha) or pleasurable?"
>
> "Painful, Lord."
>
> "But is it fit to consider that which is impermanent, dukkha, of a nature to change, as 'This is mine, this am I, this is my self'?"
>
> "It is not, Lord."

We then read that the Buddha asked the same concerning the other four khandhas. The Buddha continued:

> "Wherefore, monks, whatever is rūpa [1], past, future, present, or internal or external, or gross or subtle, or low or excellent, whether it is far or near– all rūpa should, by means of right understanding, be seen, as it really is, thus: This is not mine, this am I not, this is not my self..."

We then read that the Buddha said the same about the other four khandhas. After that the Buddha said:

[1] The text has "body", but I prefer to retain the Pāli term rūpa, since rūpakkhandha includes all paramattha dhammas which are rūpas, those of which the body consists as well as those outside. The body as a whole is a concept.

> "Seeing in this way, monks, the instructed disciple of the ariyans disregards body and he disregards feeling and he disregards perception and he disregards the habitual tendencies and he disregards consciousness; disregarding he is dispassionate; through dispassion he is freed; in freedom the knowledge comes to be: 'I am freed, and he knows: Destroyed is birth, lived is the Brahma-faring, done is what was to be done, there is no more of being such or such.' "
>
> Thus spoke the Lord; delighted, the group of five monks rejoiced in what the Lord had said. Moreover, while this discourse was being uttered, the minds of the group of five monks were freed from the cankers without grasping. At that time there were six perfected ones in the world.

While the five monks were listening they were mindful and they developed right understanding of all realities appearing through the six doors. When they were hearing Dhamma they clearly understood hearing as an element which experiences sound, which is non-self. They clearly understood sound as only a kind of rūpa which can be heard. They penetrated the truth of non-self to such degree that they attained arahatship. They could do so after they had listened only for a short time because they had accumulated wisdom already during innumerable past lives. Ordinary people need to listen, to study and to consider the true nature of nāma and rūpa for a long time. Ignorance and wrong view are deeply accumulated and even when there is intellectual understanding of realities, the wrong view of self cannot be eradicated.

If we do not understand the five khandhas as they are, we are bound to take them for self. We read in the scriptures about "personality belief", in Pāli: sakkāya diṭṭhi. We read, for example in the "Middle Length Sayings" (I, 44, Lesser Discourse of the Miscellany) that the lay follower Visākha asked the nun Dhammadinnā different questions on Dhamma and one of these was how there comes to be personality belief. Dhammadinnā answered:

> In this case, friend Visākha, an uninstructed average person, taking no count of the pure ones, not skilled in the

> dhamma of the pure ones, untrained in the dhamma of the pure ones, taking no count of the true men, not skilled in the dhamma of the true men[2], untrained in the dhamma of the true men, regards rūpa as self or self as having rūpa or rūpa as in self or self as in rūpa...

The same is said with regard to the other khandhas. When there is personality belief someone takes each of the five khandhas for self, or he may see "self" as the owner of the khandhas, or as their container, or as contained within them. The four kinds of wrong interpretation of reality which were just mentioned pertain to each of the five khandhas and thus there are twenty kinds of personality belief [3].

There are many kinds of wrong view with regard to the five khandhas. When someone clings to the belief in a self who will last forever, to the eternity view, he fails to see that what we take for self are only nāma and rūpa which fall away after they have arisen. When someone clings to the belief in a self who will be annihilated after death, to the annihilation view, he fails to see that even now there are conditions for the arising of nāma and rūpa and that thus also after death there will be conditions for their arising. The dying-consciousness is succeeded immediately by the rebirth-consciousness of the next life.

In the "Discourse on the Characteristic of Non-Self" quoted above, we read that the Buddha said to the monks: "But is it fit to consider that which is impermanent, dukkha, of a nature to change, as 'This is mine, this am I, this is my self'?" This phrase, often recurring in the scriptures, is deep in meaning. "This is mine" implies craving which appropriates things as the property of self. "This am I" implies conceit, the tendency to cling to the importance of self or compare oneself. "This is myself" is a formulation of the personality view, the belief in an abiding self, subsequently identified with the five khandhas. We learn from the Abhidhamma that craving may arise with wrong view or without it. We may, for example, think of "my arms and

[2] In Pāli: sappurisa, which term denotes the disciple of the Buddha who has realized the truth.

[3] See also the Dhammsasaṇgani, Book III, § 1003, Theory of Individuality, which is here the translation of sakkāya diṭṭhi. This term is in the suttas sometimes translated as "person-pack view".

legs" with attachment, without there necessarily being wrong view. We should know that there is not wrong view all the time when we think of ourselves. Conceit accompanies lobha-mūlacitta, citta rooted in attachment. At the moment of conceit there cannot be wrong view at the same time. The ariyans who are not arahats may still have conceit; they have eradicated wrong view but they may still cling to the importance of self or compare themselves with others.

Only right understanding of all realities appearing in daily life can eradicate the wrong view of self. When understanding has not been developed there is clinging to an idea of "I see" or "I hear". Realities such as seeing or hearing arise because of their appropriate conditions, they do not belong to anyone. We cannot do anything about them, they are beyond control.

We read in the "Greater Discourse on the Simile of the Elephant's Footprint" (Middle Length Sayings I, 28) that Sāriputta gave a Dhamma discourse to the monks. He spoke about the four noble Truths and stated that the five khandhas are dukkha. He explained that the four Great Elements are impermanent and dukkha. Then he spoke about the conditions for the arising of seeing. We read that Sāriputta said:

> Your reverences, just as a space that is enclosed by stakes and creepers and grass and clay is known as a dwelling, so a space that is enclosed by bones and sinews and flesh and skin is known as a material shape. If, your reverences, the eye that is internal is intact but external rūpa does not come within its range and there is no appropriate impact, then there is no appearance of the appropriate class of consciousness. But when, your reverences, the eye that is internal is intact and external rūpa comes within its range and there is the appropriate impact, then there is thus an appearance of the appropriate class of consciousness...

When the rūpa which is visible object impinges on the rūpa which is eyesense there are conditions for seeing-consciousness. Visible object arises and falls away in a group of rūpas, the four Great Elements and other rūpas, but only the rūpa which is visible object can contact the eyesense and can then be seen. Seeing which experiences visible object seems to last for a while, but in reality it falls away immediately. Because of the cetasika saññā, perception or remembrance, we remember concepts of people and things and since we keep on thinking about them, the falling away of seeing is bound to be covered up by thinking. When there is wrong view one takes visible object for a person or a thing. Through right understanding visible object can be known as visible object, a kind of rūpa, and seeing can be known as seeing, a type of nāma. Seeing is vipākacitta, the result of kamma. Seeing which arises because of conditions is beyond control, non-self.

Further on in the above quoted sutta we read that Sāriputta explained in the same way the conditions for the experiences through the ear and the other doorways. We cannot control which kamma produces which vipāka, kamma is anattā and vipāka is anattā. We are inclined to think of situations, for example, of losing possessions or of meeting particular people, as vipāka. A situation is not an ultimate reality. Each situation can be analysed into different sense impressions, which are vipākacittas, and moments of thinking which are not vipāka but kusala cittas or akusala cittas. When sitting in a car, we may be afraid of an accident, but if there is right understanding of kamma and vipāka, there will be less fear. When it is the appropriate moment for kamma to produce vipāka, vipākacitta will arise. If we do not go by car we may receive unpleasant sense impressions somewhere else. The sotāpanna has realized all stages of insight before he attained enlightenment. As explained before, the first stage is clearly knowing the difference between the characteristic of nāma and the characteristic of rūpa. The second stage is understanding nāma and rūpa as conditioned realities. This is not thinking of the conditions for the nāma and rūpa which appear, it is the understanding which is the result of direct awareness of nāma and rūpa as they appear in daily life. When we see, we may, for example, think, "This is vipāka", but thinking is not the keen understanding which arises when there is awareness of seeing at the present moment.

If there is no clear understanding of kamma and vipāka as anattā there is bound to be fear of losing possessions or dear people. Fear is conditioned by attachment to the pleasant feeling we derive from our possessions or from the company of dear people. Fear of death stems from anxiety about what will happen to the "self" after death, thus anxiety about what does not exist.

We read in the "Gradual Sayings" (Book of the Fours, Ch XIX, Fourth Fifty, § 4, Fearless) that the brāhmin Jaṇussoni said to the Buddha that anyone who is subject to death has fear at the thought to death. The Buddha explained that someone may be afraid, but that there are also people who have no fear of death. We read that the Buddha said:

> "In this case, brāhmin, a certain one is not freed from passions, not freed from lusts, not freed from desire, affection, from thirst and fever, not freed from craving. Then a grievous sickness afflicts such a one. Thus afflicted by grievous sickness it occurs to him: Alas! the passions that I love will leave me, or I shall leave the passions that I love. Thereupon he grieves and wails, laments and beats the breast and falls into utter bewilderment. This one, brāhmin, being subject to death, is afraid, he falls a-trembling at the thought of death.
>
> Again, brāhmin, here a certain one who regards body is not freed from lusts... is not freed from craving. Then a grievous sickness afflicts him. Thus afflicted it occurs to him: Alas! the body that I love will leave me, or I shall leave the body that I love. Thereupon he grieves... and falls into utter bewilderment. This one, brāhmin, being subject to death, is afraid, he falls a-trembling at the thought of death.
>
> Yet again, brāhmin, here a certain one has done no lovely deed, has done no profitable deed, has given no shelter to the timid; he has done evil, cruel, wrongful deeds. Then a grievous sickness afflicts such a one. Thus afflicted by grievous sickness it occurs to him: Alas! I have done no lovely deed, I have done no profitable deed, I have given no shelter to the timid. I have done evil, cruel, wrongful deeds. To the doom of those who do such deeds hereafter I am going. Thereupon he grieves ... and falls into utter

> bewilderment. This one, brāhmin, being subject to death is afraid, he falls a-trembling at the thought of death.
>
> Yet again, brāhmin, here a certain one is doubtful, full of perplexity, has come to no conclusion as to true dhamma. He grieves and wails, laments and beats the breast and falls into utter bewilderment. This one also, being subject to death, is afraid, he falls a-trembling at the thought of death...
>
> Thus these four, being subject to death, are afraid..."

The Buddha then explained that the person who is freed from desire, who does not cling to the body, who has done wholesome deeds and who is free from doubt with regard to the Dhamma is not afraid at the thought of death. We read about the person who is freed from doubt:

> "Once more, brāhmin, here a certain one is not doubtful, is not full of perplexity, has come to a conclusion as to true dhamma. Then a grievous sickness afflicts him. Thus afflicted by grievous sickness it occurs to him: Surely I have no doubt, I have no worry, I have come to a conclusion as to true dhamma. Thus he grieves not, wails not, nor beats the breast, nor falls into utter bewilderment thereat.
>
> This one, brāhmin, though subject to death, fears not, falls not a-trembling at the thought of death. So these are the four who fear not."
>
> "It is wonderful, worthy Gotama! It is marvellous, worthy Gotama! May the worthy Gotama accept me as one who has gone to him for refuge from this day forth so long as life may last."

We read that the person who is free from doubt has no fear of death. The person who has attained the first stage of enlightenment, the sotāpanna, has eradicated doubt with regard to the Dhamma. He has no doubt as to the four noble Truths, he has no doubt as to the truth that all realities are anattā. Doubt can be eliminated by the study of the Dhamma, by discussions about it, by considering the Dhamma and above all by direct understanding and mindfulness of nāma and rūpa. Right understanding has to be developed during one's activities, no matter one is cleaning one's house, washing one's cloths, preparing food or eating it. Some people believe that one's daily activities are a hindrance to the development of right understanding but there is no need to delay its development. If someone knows that paramattha dhammas, nāma and rūpa, are the objects of mindfulness and right understanding, there are conditions for the arising of mindfulness at any time.

We read in the "Gradual Sayings" (Book of the Sixes, Ch II, § 9, Mindfulness of Death) that the Buddha said to the monks that mindfulness of death is very fruitful, that it leads to the deathless, which is nibbāna. Different monks spoke about the way they were mindful of death. We read:

> "Herein, lord, such is my thought: Were I to live but one day and night, and I were to ponder over the word of the Exalted One[4] , much would be done by me— thus, lord, I make mindfulness of death become".
>
> And another said: "I too, lord, make mindfulness become."
>
> "How so, monk?"
>
> "Herein, lord, such is my thought: Were I to live for a day only, and I were to ponder over the word of the Exalted One, much would be done by me..."
>
> And another said: "Such is my thought: Were I to live long enough to eat one alms-meal..." And another: "... to munch and swallow four or five morsels..." And another: "... to munch and swallow only one morsel..."
>
> And another said: "I too, lord, make mindfulness of death become."
>
> "How so, monk?"

[4]The P.T.S. translation has here: Were I day and night to abide mindful of the Exalted One's word... Instead of this I prefer the the translation of an almost identical sutta in "The Book of the Eights", Ch VIII, § 3, Mindfulness of Death.

> "Lord, such is my thought: Were I to live long enough to breathe in after breathing out, or to breathe out after breathing in, and I were to ponder over the word of the Exalted One, much would be done by me– thus, lord, I make mindfulness of death become."
>
> And when he had thus spoken, the Exalted One said to the monks:
>
> "Monks, the monk who makes mindfulness of death become thus: 'Were I to live but one day and night and I were to ponder over the word of the Exalted One ...' or he who thinks thus: 'Were I to live for a day only ...' or ' long enough to eat one almsmeal...' or "long enough to munch and swallow four or five morsels ..., and I were to ponder over the word of the Exalted One, much would be done by me'— those monks are said to live indolently; slackly they make mindfulness of death become for the destruction of the cankers.
>
> But the monk who makes mindfulness of death become thus: 'Were I to live long enough to munch and swallow one morsel...' and he who thinks thus: 'Were I to live long enough to breathe in after breathing out, or to breathe out after breathing in, and I were to ponder over the word of the Exalted One, much would be done by me'— those monks are said to live earnestly; keenly they make mindfulness become for the destruction of the cankers.
>
> Wherefore, monks, train yourselves thus:
>
> We will live earnestly; keenly will we make mindfulness of death become for the destruction of the cankers. Train yourselves thus, monks."

Death can come at any moment . Only the monk who realizes that the time to develop right understanding is short, even as short as it takes to eat one morsel of food, or as short as it takes to breathe in or to breathe out, and that he therefore should not waste his time, is diligent. The Buddha said, "Train yourselves thus". If someone reads these words with wrong understanding he will believe that there is a self who can control the arising of mindfulness. The Buddha explained time and again that all realities are non-self and thus also mindfulness and understanding. He did not have to repeat this truth each time he gave a discourse. The monks had no misunderstanding about the Buddha's words. They were a condition for them to be mindful of whatever reality appeared.

This sutta can remind us to develop right understanding of realities even when we are eating. What we call morsel of food consists of the four Great Elements and other rūpas. Through touch the rūpas which are hardness, softness, heat or cold may appear. They arise because of conditions and appear just for a moment. They are ultimate realities which can be object of mindfulness without having to name them or to think about them. Flavour is another kind of rūpa which is experienced through the tongue by the citta which tastes. The rūpa which is flavour is different from the nāma which experiences it. Tasting is a type of vipākacitta experiencing an object through the tongue. At that moment there is no like or dislike. When the food we are eating is delicious, lobha, attachment, is likely to arise, and when the food is unappetizing anger, dosa, may arise. Dosa may appear in angry speech. Feeling arises at each moment, it can be pleasant, unpleasant or indifferent. Feeling is a type of nāma, non-self, and if we learn to be aware of it we will be less inclined to cling to an idea of "I feel". The cetasika which is remembrance, saññā, arises each moment, but usually we are forgetful of it. Because of saññā we recognize what food we are eating, we remember how to use knife, fork and spoon. No matter what we are doing there are five khandhas arising and falling away. The classification of conditioned realities as five khandhas, one rūpakkhandha and four nāma-kkhandhas, can remind us not to be forgetful of what appears. There are the khandha of feeling and the khandha of remembrance all the time, but if we are never aware of them we will continue to take them for self. Apart from feeling and saññā, there are other cetasikas, classified as the khandha of "mental formations", saṅkhārakkhandha. Good qualities and bad qualities are included in saṅkhārakkhandha. Awareness of nāma and rūpa is not trying to find out which khandha a particular reality is. The classification of conditioned realities as one rūpa-kkhandha and four nāma-kkhandhas can remind us of the difference between nāma and rūpa. All realities which are rūpakkhandha do not experience anything, they have no sensitivity, whereas the realities which are classified as the four nāma-kkhandhas are realities which experience something. Feeling is an experience, saññā is another experience, cetasikas such as lobha or dosa, classified as sankhārakkhandha, are experiences, and cittas are experiences. In order to realize nāma and rūpa which appear at this moment as anattā, we have to understand first of all the difference between the reality which does not experience anything and the reality which is an experience. If we do not distinguish between the characteristics of nāma and rūpa, we will continue to cling to a self. The clinging to a self is the cause of a great deal of worry and disturbance. When we suffer from painful feeling or sickness we are inclined to think of a self who suffers. In reality there are only the five khandhas which arise just for a moment and fall away. We read in the "Kindred Sayings" (III, Khandhā-vagga, Kindred Sayings on Elements, First Fifty, Ch 5, § 43, An Island to Oneself [5] that the Buddha said:

> Monks, be islands unto yourselves, be your own refuge, having no other; let the Dhamma be an island and a refuge to you, having no other. Those who are islands unto themselves... should investigate to the very heart of things: "What is the source of sorrow, lamentation, pain, grief and despair? How do they arise?"
>
> Here, monks, the uninstructed worldling, with no regard for the Noble Ones... regards body as the self, the self as having body, body as being in the self, or the self as being in the body. Change occurs in this man's body, and it becomes different. On account of this change and difference, sorrow, lamentation, pain, grief and despair arise.
>
> (Similarly with feelings, perceptions, mental formations, consciousness.)

[5] I am using the translation by Walshe, in Samyutta Nikāya, An Anthology, Part III, Wheel, 318- 321, Kandy.

But seeing the body's impermanence, its changeability, its waning, its ceasing, he says, "formerly as now, all bodies were impermanent and unsatisfactory, and subject to change." Thus, seeing this as it really is, with perfect insight, he abandons all sorrow, lamentation, pain, grief and despair. He is not worried at their abandonment, but unworriedly lives at ease, and thus living at ease he is said to be "assuredly delivered".

(Similarly with feelings, perceptions, mental formations, consciousness.)

Chapter 4

The Daily Life of the Monk

We read in the Commentary of the "Theragātha" (Psalms of the Brethren) that Jenta was wondering whether he would leave the world. After he heard the Buddha preach he entered the order and attained arahatship. We read in Canto CXI, Jenta, the following verse uttered by him [1]:

> Hard is the life without the world, and hard
> In truth to bear house life. Deep is the Dhamma;
> Hard too is wealth to win. Thus difficult
> The choice between the life of monk or layman[2].
> I ought to bear unceasingly in mind
> (And see in everything) impermanence.

The life of laymen is difficult, they have to exert themselves to earn their living. The monk's life is also difficult, he is dependant on laymen for the obtainment of the four requisites of robes, food, dwelling and medicines. No matter whether someone is monk or layman, he experiences objects through the six doors, and on account of these objects attachment tends to arise. If one does not develop

[1] I slightly modified the P.T.S. translation by Mrs. Rhys Davids, in order to make it more readable.

[2] The translation has: The choice of one or other how to live.

satipaṭṭhāna, defilements will increase evermore and thus life will become more and more difficult. Jenta did not merely think, "Everything is impermanent". Thinking about impermanence is not the same as the penetration of the characteristic of impermanence, of the arising and falling away of each reality which appears. The Dhamma is subtle and deep. Although the Dhamma is near, we do not understand it: we do not understand seeing which appears now or hearing which appears now; they arise and fall away, they are impermanent. Jenta had developed vipassanā and he had penetrated the three characteristics of impermanence, dukkha and anattā of all realities which appeared in his daily life. Otherwise he could not have attained arahatship. Even a short reminder of impermanence, as we find in Jenta's verse, is very beneficial, it can be a condition for us not to delay awareness of the nāma or rūpa appearing at this moment. In order to realize the arising and falling away of nāma and rūpa vipassanā has to be developed stage by stage, but it is of no use to worry about the difficulty of its development. We should begin at the present moment, be it seeing, hearing or thinking.

One may find it difficult to be mindful of realities while one is working, while one is in a hurry or while one is speaking. Not only laypeople, but also monks have many tasks to perform. It is very useful to read about the monks' daily life in the Vinaya[3]. The monks had to sweep around their dwelling places, they had to clean their dwellings, they had to wash their robes, but they had to perform their tasks with mindfulness of nāma and rūpa. We read in the "Book of Discipline" (IV, Ch II, Observance, 118):

> Now at that time the Observance-hall in a certain residence came to be soiled. Incoming monks looked down upon, criticised, spread it about, saying: "How can these monks not sweep the Observance-hall?" They told this matter to the Lord. He said: "I allow you, monks, to sweep the Observance-hall."

The Buddha had to give the monks permission to perform such tasks as sweeping or cleaning, but he would not have given them

[3]Translated as 6 volumes of "The Book of the Discipline", in the P. T. S. edition.

permission to do these chores if mindfulness during their work was impossible. The Vinaya is the "Middle Way"; the observance of the rules should go together with the development of right understanding of whatever reality naturally appears in daily life.

We read in the "Kindred Sayings"(IV, Part II, Kindred Sayings about Feeling, 3, § 26) that the Buddha said:

> There are these three feelings, monks. What three? Pleasant feeling, painful feeling, neutral feeling.
>
> Whatsoever recluses or brahmins [4] understand not as they really are the arising, the destruction, the satisfaction and misery of, the escape from, these three feelings, those recluses and brahmins are approved neither among recluses as recluses nor among brahmins as brahmins. And those venerable ones have not understood of themselves, have not realized, the profit of being recluses or brahmins, nor have they lived in the attainment thereof.
>
> But those recluses and brahmins who have done so, are approved both among recluses as recluses and among brahmins as brahmins. And those venerable ones have understood of themselves, have realized, the profit of being recluses or brahmins, and having so attained do live in the present life.

Feeling arises with each moment of citta but we are usually unaware of the different feelings. The monks who were not mindful and did not understand the true nature of feeling, as impermanent, dukkha and anattā, were not approved of. In order to be a true recluse they should develop right understanding of nāma and rūpa.

We read in the "Gradual Sayings"(II, Book of the Fours, Ch II §2, Virtue)[5]:

---

[4]In Pāli: brāhmaṇa, referring not only to a member of the Brahman caste, but also to someone who leads a pure life.

[5]I am using the tramnslation by Ven. Nyanaponika, in Anguttara Nikāya, An Anthology I, Wheel 155-158, B.P.S. Kandy.

> Devoted to virtue you should dwell, O monks, devoted to the discipline of the Order and restrained by that discipline! Perfect be your conduct and behaviour! Seeing danger even in the smallest transgression, you should train yourselves in the rules which you have accepted! But if a monk lives like that, what should he further do?
>
> If a monk, while walking, standing, sitting or reclining, is free from greed and hatred, from sloth and torpor, from restlessness and worry, and has discarded sceptical doubt, then his will[6] has become strong and impregnable; his mindfulness is alert and unclouded; his body calm and unexcited; his mind concentrated and collected.
>
> A monk who in such a manner ever and again shows earnest endeavour and moral shame, is called energetic and resolute.
>
> Controlled when walking, standing, sitting and reclining,
> Controlled in bending, stretching of the limbs,
> Careful observer of the world around him:
> He knows how khandhas arise and cease.
> He who thus lives with ardent mind
> And calm demeanour, free from restlessness,
> Who trains himself in quietude of mind,
> With constancy and perseverance—
> As "Ever-resolute" that monk is known.

In the "Mahā-satipaṭṭhāna sutta" (Dialogues of the Buddha II, no. 22) and in the "Satipaṭṭhāna sutta" (Middle Length Sayings I, no. 10) the Buddha also explained that the monk should practise "clear comprehension", sati and right understanding, in all postures. When we read in the above-quoted translation the word "controlled", we should remember that there is no self who controls; the word "controlled" implies mindfulness of realities. We are walking, standing, sitting or reclining, bending and stretching during the day, and at all those moments realities are appearing through the six doors. Right

[6] The P.T.S. edition has here: energy.

understanding can be developed no matter what one is doing. When we read about the tasks the monks had to perform we can read such passages with right understanding of the goal of monkhood: the development of right understanding to the degree of arahatship. The Buddha did not have to repeat all the time: "do your tasks with mindfulness", because he had explained this already.

In the beginning the Buddha had not laid down rules of conduct, but when monks deviated from their purity of life there was an occasion to lay down rules. We read in the "Book of Discipline"(I, Suttavibhaṅga, Defeat I, 9) that Sāriputta said to the Buddha:

> "It is the right time, lord, it is the right time, well-farer, at which the lord should make known the course of training for disciples and should appoint the Pāṭimokkha, in order that this Brahma-life may persist and last long."
>
> "Wait, Sāriputta, wait, Sāriputta. The tathāgata will know the right time for that. The teacher does not make known, Sāriputta, the course of training for disciples, or appoint the Pāṭimokkha until some conditions causing the cankers appear here in the Order. And as soon, Sāriputta, as some conditions causing the cankers appear here in the Order, then the teacher makes known the course of training for disciples, he appoints the Pāṭimokkha in order to ward off those conditions causing the cankers....

The rules of Pāṭimokkha, a collection of precepts, were recited twice a month. We read about the purposes of the rules the monks had to observe in the "Gradual Sayings" (Book of the Twos, Ch XVII, § 1, Results):

> Monks, it was to bring about these pairs of results that the Observances were enjoined on his disciples by the Tathāgata. What two?
>
> The excellence and well-being of the Order...
>
> The control of ill-conditioned monks and the comfort of good monks...

> The restraint, in this very life, of the āsavas, guilt, faults, fears and unprofitable states: and the protection against the same in a future life.
>
> Out of compassion for householders, and to uproot the factions of the evilly disposed...
>
> To give confidence to believers, and for the betterment of believers...
>
> To establish true Dhamma, for the support of the Discipline...
>
> Monks, it was to bring about these pairs of results...

As we read, one of the results is the restraint of the āsavas, all defilements. The rules help the monk to be mindful and to develop right understanding in order to eradicate all defilements. The rules for the monk should not be separated from the development of satipaṭṭhāna.

We read in the "Book of Discipline"(III, Suttavibhaṅga, Training, 195) about a group of six monks who had bad manners while eating. We read:

> ... Now at that time the group of six monks, while eating, put the whole hand into the mouth...
>
> "I will not put the whole hand into the mouth while eating," is a training to be observed."
>
> One should not put the whole hand into the mouth while eating. Whoever out of disrespect puts the whole hand into the mouth while eating, there is an offence of wrong-doing.
>
> There is no offence if it is unintentional, if he is not thinking, if he does not know, if he is ill... if he is mad, if he is the first wrong-doer....

We read time and again, when there is reference to a bad deed, that the Buddha asked whether the person who did a bad deed had the intention or volition to do such a deed. He should scrutinize himself as to this. From the Abhidhamma we learn that akusala kamma is actually unwholesome intention, akusala cetanā cetasika. We read that there is no offence when someone is the first wrong-doer. The reason is that at that moment there is no rule yet which can be transgressed.

Further on we read about other rules, given on account of bad manners of the "group of six monks". We read, for example, about the following rules:

> "...I will not talk with a mouthful in the mouth," is a training to be observed...
>
> "...I will not eat tossing up balls (of food)," is a training to be observed...
>
> "...I will not eat stuffing the cheeks," is a training to be observed...
>
> "...I will not eat smacking the lips," is a training to be observed...
>
> "...I will not eat making a hissing sound," is a training to be observed...
>
> "...I will not eat licking the fingers," is a training to be observed...
>
> "...I will not eat licking the bowl," is a training to be observed...

These are only a few examples of rules of conduct to be observed while eating. The monk should see danger in the smallest faults. When he is mindful of nāma and rūpa also while eating he will not eat thoughtlessly. The almsfood he receives is a gift of the faithful layfollowers and he should be worthy of this gift. It should remind him of the obligation of striving after the goal of monkhood. When the food is delicious lobha is likely to arise, but he can be mindful of lobha and realize it as only a type of nāma.

We read in the "Book of Discipline"(IV, Mahāvagga, I, The Great Section, 45-54) about rules concerning the conduct of the newly ordained monk towards his preceptor, a person who gives guidance to him. We read:

> "Monks, I allow a preceptor. The preceptor, monks, should arouse in the one who shares his cell the attitude of a son;

> the one who shares his cell should arouse in the preceptor the attitude of a father. Thus these, living with reverence, with deference, with courtesy towards one another, will come to growth, to increase, to maturity in this dhamma and discipline..."

Here, the Buddha reminds the monks again of the purpose of the rules: growth and maturity in this "dhamma and discipline". The pupil has to perform many tasks for the preceptor, but not without mindfulness of nāma and rūpa. We read:

> "The one who shares a cell, monks, should conduct himself properly towards the preceptor. This is the proper conduct in this repect: having got up early, having taken off his sandals, having arranged his upper robe over one shoulder, he should give tooth-wood, he should give water for rinsing the mouth, he should make ready a seat. If there is conjey[7], having washed the bowl, the conjey should be placed near (the preceptor). When he has drunk the conjey, having given him water, having received the bowl, having lowered it, having washed it properly without rubbing it, it should be put away. When the preceptor has got up, the seat should be removed. If that place is soiled, that place should be swept...

Further on we read about many other tasks the newly ordained monk had to perform for his preceptor. He should prepare a bath for him, and arrange for everything the preceptor needs in the bathroom. He should clean the dwelling place and sweep it when it is soiled. He should open the windows by day if the weather is cool and close them at night. If the wheather is warm, he should close the windows by day and open them at night. He should not only look after the preceptor's material needs, but he should also help him as regards his spiritual needs. We read (49):

[7] Rice gruel

> If dissatisfaction has arisen in the preceptor, the one who shares his cell should allay it or should get (another) to allay it, or he should give him a talk on dhamma. If remorse has arisen in the preceptor, the one who shares the cell should dispel it, or he should give him a talk on dhamma. If wrong views have arisen in the preceptor, the one who shares the cell should dissuade him (from them) or should get (another) to dissuade him (from them), or he should give him a talk on dhamma...

We then read about the obligations of the preceptor towards the monk who shares his cell. He should help him with regard to the recitation of the texts, exhort and instruct him. He should also help him in material way and look after him when he is sick.

Reading the details about the many tasks the monks had to perform in their daily life is useful for laypeople as well. The Buddha exhorted the monks to develop satipaṭṭhāna during all their activities and this can remind laypeople that, no matter what they are doing, there are realities appearing through the six doors which can be objects of mindfulness. There are nāma and rūpa when one cleans one's house, open and close windows or look after sick relatives. The Vinaya does not contain merely rules, but also discourses in which the Buddha explained about absolute realities which can be objects of mindfulness and right understanding. There is also Abhidhamma in the Vinaya; the Buddha explained about the four noble Truths, about the five khandhas, about all the objects impinging on the six doors. Thus, the Vinaya, the Suttanta and the Abhidhamma are in conformity with each other.

We read in the Book of Discipline (IV, Mahāvagga, I, The Great Section, 21) that the Buddha, while he was staying near Gaya with thousand monks who had formerly been "matted hair ascetics", addressed these monks:

> Monks, everything is burning. And what, monks, is everything that is burning? The eye, monks, is burning, visible objects are burning, seeing-consciousness is burning, eye-contact is burning, in other words the feeling which

arises from eye-contact, be it pleasant or painful or neither painful nor pleasant, that too is burning. With what is it burning? I say it is burning with the fire of passion, with the fire of hatred, with the fire of stupidity; it is burning because of birth, ageing, dying, because of grief, sorrow, suffering, lamentation and despair.

The ear... sounds... the nose... odours... the tongue... tastes... the body... tangible objects... the mind... mental states... mind-consciousness is burning, mind-contact is burning, in other words the feeling which arises through mind-contact, be it pleasant or painful or neither painful nor pleasant, that too is burning. With what is it burning? I say it is burning with the fire of passion, with the fire of hatred, with the fire of stupidity; it is burning because of birth, ageing, dying, because of grief, sorrow, suffering, lamentation and despair.

Seeing this, monks, the instructed disciple of the ariyans disregards the eye and he disregards visible objects and he disregards seeing-consciousness and he disregards eye-contact, in other words the feeling which arises from eye-contact, be it pleasant or painful or neither painful nor pleasant, that too he disregards. And he disregards the ear... sounds... the nose... odours... the tongue... tastes... the body... tangible objects... the mind... mental states... mind-consciousness... mind-contact, in other words the feeling that arises from mind-contact, be it pleasant or painful or neither painful nor pleasant, that too he disregards; disregarding, he is dispassionate; through dispassion he is freed; in freedom the knowledge comes to be, "I am freed", and he comprehends: Destroyed is birth, lived is the Brahma-faring, done is what was to be done, there is no more of being such or such."

And while this discourse was being uttered, the minds of these thousand monks were freed from the cankers without grasping.

In this passage the Buddha taught Abhidhamma: he taught about cittas experiencing objects through the six doors, he taught about cetasikas such as contact, feeling, lobha (attachment), dosa (aversion) and moha (ignorance), and he taught about rūpas such as the sense objects and the senses; in short, he taught about absolute realities. He showed the danger of lobha, dosa, and moha, which arise on account of what is experienced through the six doors. So long as there are defilements there will be birth, old age, sickness and death, and all the suffering inherent in the cycle of birth and death. Right understanding of each reality which appears leads to detachment. The monks who listened were mindful of seeing, visible object, hearing, sound, of all nāmas and rūpas which appeared at that moment. We tend to cling to ourselves, we think of the body as if it belongs to us, we think of our eyes, ears, arms and legs, and we forget the conditions from which it originates. The rūpas we call our body are rūpas produced by the four factors of kamma, citta, food and temperature. No matter we walk, stand, sit or lie down, bend or stretch, the rūpas of the body which arise and fall away are produced by these four factors. A dead body cannot move, there are only rūpas produced by temperature. We are inclined to forget that earsense is a particular rūpa in the ear produced by kamma throughout our life, and that it arises and falls away. Earsense can only be contacted by sound. Sound is a rupa which can be heard by hearing-consciousness. We are inclined to take hearing for self but we can verify that it is a type of nāma arisen because of its appropriate conditions. The monks who listened developed right understanding even to the degree of arahatship. They were freed from birth.

The goal of monkhood is arahatship and therefore the monks who were not arahats yet had to listen to the teachings, consider them and develop satipaṭṭhāna. They recited the Buddha's teachings, they held Dhamma discussions and they taught the Dhamma. We read in the "Dialogues of the Buddha"(III, no. 29, The Delectable Discourse) that the Buddha said to Cunda that he, the Buddha, had come to his journey's end, but that there were senior monks who were well trained, who had attained arahatship and were able to propagate the Dhamma. He said that there were also monks of middle age and standing who were his disciples and who were wise. He said that among his disciples there were also novices, sisters, laymen and laywomen. His religion (brahmacariya, the "brahman life") was in every way successful, complete, well set forth in all its full extent. Further on the Buddha said to Cunda:

> Wherefore, Cunda, do you, to whom I have made known the truths that I have perceived, come together in company and rehearse all of you together those doctrines and quarrel not over them, but compare meaning with meaning, and phrase with phrase, in order that this pure religion may last long and be perpetuated, in order that it may continue to be for the good and happiness of the great multitudes, out of love for the world, to the good and the gain and the happiness of devas and men!

It was the task of the Sangha, the Order of monks, to preserve the teachings and to hand them on to future generations. Many of the Buddha's disciples had attained arahatship and among them Sāriputta and Moggallāna were the Buddha's chief disciples. They were called by the Buddha "model and standard" for the other monks. Sāriputta, who was called the "marshall of the Dhamma" was the guardian of the welfare of the monks [8]. With his penetrative understanding and ability to teach he explained in detail the sermons which the Buddha had preached in brief. The systematization of the Abhidhamma texts also originated with Sāriputta [9]. Sāriputta and Moggallāna had passed away before the Buddha and thus they did not attend the Great Council which was held at Rājagaha, shortly after the Buddha's passing away. We read in the "Expositor" (Atthasālinī I, Introductory Discourse, 27):

> Thus at the time of the Rehearsal at the First Council, held by the five hundred, the company of the self-controlled[10],

[8] See "The Life of Sāriputta" by Ven. Nyanaponika, Wheel no. 90-92, B.P.S. Kandy.

[9] See Ch 1.

[10] Arahats.

who recited under the presidency of Mahā Kassapa did so after previous determination: "This is the Dhamma, this is the Vinaya[11]"; these are the first words, these the middle words, these the later words of the Buddha; this is the Vinaya-Piṭaka, this the Suttanta-Piṭaka, this the Abhidhamma-Piṭaka, this the Dīgha Nikāya (Dialogues of the Buddha), the Majjhima Nikāya (Middle Length Sayings), the Saṃyutta Nikāya (Kindred Sayings), the Anguttara Nikāya (Gradual Sayings), the Khuddaka Nikāya (Minor Collection); these the nine parts, to wit, the Suttas, etc.[12]; these the eighty-four thousand units of text."

All this was rehearsed in seven months. Mahā Kassapa interrogated Upāli, a monk who knew the Vinaya by heart, on the entire Vinaya. After that he interrogated Ānanda on the rest of the teachings[13]. Ānanda, who had been the Buddha's personal attendant during his last twentyfive years and who had attained arahatship on the eve of the Council, had a powerful memory of all that was spoken by the Buddha, even eighty-four thousand units of texts; he remembered where a sermon was spoken and on what occasion. The discourses of the first four Nikāyas start with Ānanda's words: Thus have I heard, in Pāli: Evaṃ me suttaṃ. This indicates that he only rehearsed what was spoken by the Buddha.

We read further on in the "Introductory Discourse" of the "Expositor" about the importance of understanding Abhidhamma:

> ... And tradition has it that those bhikkhus only who know Abhidhamma are true preachers of the Dhamma; the rest,

[11]The whole of the teachings is also referred to as "The Dhamma and the Vinaya".

[12]These nine parts, sometimes mentioned in the Discourses (for example, Middle Length Sayings, no. 22), are: suttas without verses and suttas with verses, expositions (veyākarana) which includes the Abhidhamma, Jātaka (Birth stories) and other parts. See for a more detailed explanation the"Expositor"I, Introductory Discourse, 25-27.

[13]See the Book of Discipline V, Cullavagga, Ch XI, and the "Illustrator of Ultimate Meaning", commentary to the "Good Omen Discourse" of the "Minor Readings", Khuddaka Nikāya.

> though they speak on the Dhamma, are not preachers thereof. And why? They, in speaking on the Dhamma, confuse the different kinds of Kamma and of its results, the distinction between nāma and rūpa, and the different kinds of dhammas. The students of Abhidhamma do not thus get confused; hence a bhikkhu who knows Abhidhamma, whether he preaches Dhamma or not, will be able to answer questions whenever asked. He alone, therefore, is a true preacher of the Dhamma.

Even today the Sangha, the Order of monks, should continue to preserve the Buddha's teachings by the study and the practice of the Dhamma.

We read in the "Gradual Sayings" (II, Book of the Fours, Fourth Fifty, Ch XVI, § 10, The Wellfarer's Discipline) that there are four things which lead to the vanishing of Saddhamma, true Dhamma: the monks learn by heart a text that is wrongly taken, the monks are incapable of being instructed, the monks who know the teachings by heart do not dutifully hand on a text, and the monks are backsliding, and do not make an effort to win the goal. We then read :

> Now, monks, these four things conduce to the support, to the non-confusion, to the not vanishing away of Saddhamma. What four?
>
> Herein the monks get by heart a text that is rightly taken, with words and sense that are rightly arranged. Now if words and sense are rightly arranged the meaning also is easy to follow...
>
> Then again the monks are easy to speak to, possessed of qualities which make them easy to speak to; they are tractable, capable of being instructed...
>
> Yet again those monks who are of wide knowledge, versed in the doctrines, who know Dhamma by heart, who know the Vinaya by heart, who know the summaries by heart,- these dutifully hand on a text to another; thus, when they

pass away, the text is not cut down at the root, it has something to stand on...

Yet again the elder monks live not in abundance, they are not lax, they take not the lead in backsliding (to the worldly life), they shirk not the burden of the secluded life, they set going an effort to reach the unattained, to win the goal not won, to realize the unrealized. So the generation that follows comes to depend upon their view. That generation also lives not in abundance... but makes an effort to realize the unrealized...

So these, monks, are the four things that conduce to the support, to the non-confusion, to the not vanishing away of Saddhamma.

Chapter 5

The Duties of the Lay-follower

The Buddha taught the Dhamma to monks, to nuns and to lay-followers, men and women. He preached to people with different ways of life and different accumulated inclinations. He knew that people who listened to him had not the same capability to grasp the Dhamma. We read in the "Kindred Sayings" (IV, Saḷāyatanavagga, Part VIII, Kindred Sayings about Headmen, § 7, Teaching):

> Once the Exalted One was staying at Nālandā, in Pāvārika Mango Grove.
>
> Then Asibandhaka's son, the headman, came to see the Exalted One, and on coming to him saluted him and sat down at one side. So seated... he said:-
>
> "Does not the Exalted One, lord, dwell in compassion for every living thing?"
>
> "Yes, headman, the Tathāgata does so dwell."
>
> "But, lord, does the Exalted One teach the Dhamma in full to certain ones, but to certain others he does not teach the Dhamma in full?"
>
> "Now, headman, as to this I shall question you. Do you reply as you think fit.

Now what do you think, headman? Suppose a yeoman farmer here has three fields, one excellent, one moderate, and one poor, hard, saltish, of bad soil. Now what do you think, headman? When that yeoman farmer wants to sow his seed, which field would he sow first, the excellent field, the moderate field, or the one that is poor, hard, saltish, of bad soil?"

"That yeoman farmer, lord, wishing to sow his seed, would first sow the excellent field, and having done so he would sow the moderate one. Having so done he might and might not sow that field that is poor, hard, saltish, of bad soil. Why so? Because in any case it might do for cattle-food."

"Well, headman, just like that excellent field are my ordained disciples, both men and women. I teach them the Dhamma that is lovely in its beginning, lovely in its middle and lovely in its ending, both in spirit and in letter. I make known to them the righteous life that is wholly perfect and utterly pure. Why is that? Because, headman, these people abide with me for their island, with me for their cave of shelter, me for their stronghold, me for their refuge.

Then, headman, just like that moderate field are my lay-disciples, both men and women. I teach them the Dhamma that is lovely in its beginning, lovely in its middle and lovely in its ending, both in spirit and in letter. I make known to them the righteous life that is wholly perfect and utterly pure. Why is that? Because, headman, these people abide with me for their island, with me for their cave and shelter, me for their stronghold, me for their refuge.

Then, headman, just like that field that is poor, hard, saltish, of bad soil, are my wandering recluses and brahmins that hold other views than mine. To them also I teach the Dhamma that is lovely in its beginning, lovely in its middle, lovely in its ending, both in spirit and in letter. I make known to them the righteous life that is wholly perfect and utterly pure. Why so? Because if they understand

> but a single sentence of it, that would be to their profit and happiness for many a long day..."

Even if someone has understood just one sentence, it might help him later on to have more understanding of the Dhamma. He might listen again to the Dhamma in a future life and then his understanding could develop. Out of compassion the Buddha continued to teach Dhamma for fortyfive years. We read in the "Dialogues of the Buddha"(II, no. XVI, The Book of the Great Decease, 113) that the Buddha related to Ānanda what he had answered to Māra when he had said to the Buddha that he should now pass away:

> And when he had thus spoken, Ānanda, I addressed Māra, the Evil One, and said:- "I shall not pass away, O Evil One! until not only the monks and nuns of the Order, but also the lay-disciples of either sex shall have become true hearers, wise and well trained, ready and learned, carrying the doctrinal books in their memory, masters of the lesser corollaries that follow from the larger doctrine, correct in life, walking according to the precepts-until they, having thus themselves learned the doctrine, shall be able to tell others of it, preach it, make it known, establish it, open it, minutely explain it and make it clear- until they, when others start vain doctrine easy to be refuted by the truth, shall be able in refuting it to spread the wonder-working truth abroad! I shall not die until this pure religion of mine shall have become successful, prosperous, wide-spread, and popular in all its full extent- until, in a word, it shall have been well proclaimed among men!"

The monks, nuns and layfollowers who listened to the Buddha and considered what he taught could develop right understanding in their daily lives. They developed understanding of paramattha dhammas, of citta, cetasika and rūpa, which are impermanent, dukkha and nonself. People may believe in a soul or mind which experiences different objects. The Buddha taught about cittas which experience different objects. Each citta which arises falls away within splitseconds, at each moment there is a different experience. We read in the "Book of Analysis" (Vibhaṅga, Ch 16, Analysis of Knowledge, Singlefold Exposition, 319, 320) about the sense-cognitions of seeing, hearing, etc., which each are dependant on a rūpa which is their physical base, the corresponding sense-base, and a rūpa which is the corresponding sense object. Thus, seeing has eyesense as its base and visible object as its object. Seeing, its base and its object fall away, they are impermanent, non-self. We read:

> "Have different bases, have different objects" means: The base and object of eye consciousness is (one thing); the base and object of ear consciousness is another; the base and object of nose consciousness is another; the base and object of tongue consciousness is another; the base and object of body consciousness is another.
>
> "Do not experience each other's object" means: Ear consciousness does not experience the object of eye consciousness; eye consciousness does not experience the object of ear consciousness either. Nose consciousness does not experience the object of eye consciousness; eye consciousness does not experience the object of nose consciousness either. Tongue consciousness does not experience the object of eye consciousness; eye consciousness does not experience the object of tongue consciousness either. Body consciousness does not experience the object of eye consciousness; eye consciousness does not experience the object of body consciousness either...

Of the other sense-cognitions it is explained in the same way that they do not experience each other's object. It is said that they do not arise in succession and that they do not arise simultaneously. It is helpful to learn more details about cittas which experience objects through the different doorways. We may find it obvious that seeing is different from hearing, but only when there is mindfulness of seeing when it appears or of hearing when it appears, understanding of what paramattha dhammas are will be clearer. In this way the idea of self who sees or hears can be eliminated. Among the people who listened to the Buddha there were kings, householders and slaves. The hearing of a king or of a slave, hearing at that time or hearing today is always the same: hearing has its own characteristic which cannot be altered. Hearing experiences only sound, not the voice of a person, or the noise of something. People who listened to the Buddha could be mindful of the paramattha dhamma appearing at the present moment and in that way right understanding of its characteristic could develop.

Sati or mindfulness is not concentration on a particular reality. One never can tell when a particular reality will arise and when there will be mindfulness. Trying to do something special in order to have sati is motivated by lobha, attachment, and this is not the right condition for sati. Understanding of paramattha dhammas and consideration of the truth are the right conditions for the arising of sati, there is no other way. Someone may think that his daily life is too busy, that he has no time to consider paramattha dhammas. He may believe that he, because of his work, has to think continuously of persons, of conventional realities. However, even thinking is a conditioned reality. We think with lobha, attachment, and dosa, aversion, there is like or dislike of objects time and again. We cannot get rid of akusala, but it can be the object of understanding. If we understand the characteristic of sati and if we understand what the object of sati is: a nama or a rūpa, it can arise naturally in daily life. It will arise sometimes, but it is natural that there are countless moments without sati. The Buddha, when he explained about the nature of non-self [1], said to the monks that one cannot say, "let body be thus for me, let body not be thus for me", and that it is the same with regard to the other four khandhas. We should remember that we cannot tell citta to be in this way, not in that way. Citta is beyond control, but it can be understood as it is.

We read in the scriptures about kings who were followers of the Buddha. These kings were very busy and they had many people around them, but they developed satipaṭṭhāna and even attained enlightenment. King Bimbisara, for example, became a sotāpanna. We read in the "Kindred Sayings"(IV, Saḷāyatanavagga, Kindred Sayings on Sense, Third Fifty, Ch 3, the Housefathers, § 127, Bhāradvāja) that

[1] See Ch 3, where I quoted from Book of Discipline IV, Mahā-vagga, 9-14).

King Udena [2] asked the venerable Piṇḍola of Bhāradvāja how young monks could overcome their passions and practise the righteous life. Piṇḍola answered that the Buddha had told them to see all women as if they were their mother, sister or daughter. When the King remarked that the heart is wanton, Piṇḍola said that the Buddha had told the monks to regard the body as full of impurities. The King said that this was hard for those who were untrained. He asked whether there was another condition for the monks to practise the righteous life. Thereupon Piṇḍola said that the Buddha had explained how the six doors are guarded by mindfulness:

> ... Seeing an object with the eye, be not misled by its outer view, nor by its lesser details. But since coveting and dejection, evil, unprofitable states, might overwhelm one who dwells with the faculty of the eye uncontrolled, do you apply yourselves to such control, set a guard over the faculty of the eye and attain control of it...

The same is said with regard to the other doorways. When one is infatuated with thoughts about people and things and there is no mindfulness, the doorways are not guarded. When there is mindfulness of visible object and when there is right understanding of it as only a rūpa which is seen, one attaches less importance to it. We learn from the Abhidhamma that visible object is one rūpa out of the twentyeight kinds of rūpa, and that it is the only rūpa which can be seen. The Abhidhamma helps us to have more understanding of the objects of mindfulness. The King understood what Piṇḍola had said about the guarding of the six doors and he praised him. He spoke about his own experiences:

> I myself, master Bhāradvāja, whenever I enter my palace with body, speech and mind unguarded, with thought unsettled, with my faculties uncontrolled,- at such times lustful states overwhelm me. But whenever, master Bhāradvāja,

[2] See Dictionary of Pāli Proper Names, by Malalasekera, P.T.S. This dictionary in two volumes gives us the details of the lives of the persons we read about in the suttas, with all the references to the corresponding parts of the scriptures. It also gives us the contents in brief of the suttas under their Pāli titles.

> I do so with body, speech and mind guarded, with thought settled, with my faculties controlled, at such times lustful states do not overwhelm me.
>
> Excellent, master Bhāradvāja! Excellent it is, master Bhāradvāja! Even as one raises what is overthrown, or shows forth what is hidden, or points out the way to him that wanders astray, or holds up a light in the darkness, so that they who have eyes may see objects,- even so in divers ways has the Dhamma been set forth by the worthy Bhāradvāja. I myself, master Bhāradvāja, do go for refuge to that Exalted One, to the Dhamma and to the Order of monks. May the worthy Bhāradvāja accept me as a follower from this day forth, so long as life lasts, as one who has so taken refuge.

The King had great confidence in the Dhamma, he could verify for himself that when there was forgetfulness akusala cittas arose and when there was mindfulness kusala cittas arose. When there are conditions for the arising of sati it arises, without the need to prepare for it. Even a short moment of sati is most beneficial, because then there can be a beginning of right understanding of realities. If there is mindfulness now we can know that this moment is different from the previous moment when there was none. Gradually we can come to understand the characteristic of sati.

Mahānāma was another king who developed satipaṭṭhāna in daily life. We read in the "Gradual Sayings" (IV, Book of the Eights, Ch III, § 5, Mahānāma, the Sakyan) that Mahānāma asked the Buddha, while he was dwelling in Banyan Tree Park, at Kapilavatthu, how a man becomes a lay-disciple. The Buddha said:

> "When, Mahānāma, he has found refuge in the Buddha, found refuge in the Dhamma, found refuge in the Order, then he is a lay-disciple."
>
> "Lord, how is a lay-disciple virtuous?"
>
> "When, Mahānāma, a lay-disciple abstains from taking life; abstains from taking what is not given him; abstains

> from lustful and evil indulgences; abstains from lying; and abstains from spirituous intoxicants, the cause of indolence- then a lay-disciple is virtuous."
>
> "Lord, how does a lay-disciple help on his own welfare, but not that of another?"
>
> "When, Mahānāma, he has achieved faith [3] for self, but strives not to compass faith in another; has achieved virtue for self, but strives not to compass virtue in another; has achieved himself renunciation, but strives not to compass renunciation in another; longs himself to see monks, but strives not for this sight for another; longs himself to hear Saddhamma [4], but strives not for this hearing for another; is mindful himself of Dhamma he has heard, but strives not that another should be mindful of it; reflects himself upon the meaning of Dhamma he is mindful of, but strives not for another to reflect thereon; when he knows himself both the letter and the spirit of Dhamma and walks in comformity therewith, but strives not for another so to walk- then a lay-disciple helps on his own welfare, but not that of another."
>
> "And how, lord, does a lay-disciple help on both his own welfare and the welfare of another?"
>
> "When indeed, Mahānāma, he has achieved faith himself and strives to compass faith in another; has achieved virtue himself... renunciation... longs to see monks... to hear Saddhamma... is mindful... reflects... when he knows both the letter and the spirit of Dhamma and walks in conformity therewith and strives to make another so to walk- then, Mahānāma, a lay-disciple helps on his own welfare and the welfare of another."

It is the task of the monks to study and explain the Dhamma, but also lay-disciples should, each in their own way, help to explain

[3] In Pāli: saddhā, which has the meaning of confidence in wholesomeness.

[4] True Dhamma.

the teachings and their application. This sutta can encourage all of us to study the Dhamma more, to consider the Dhamma more, and, even though we are beginners on the Path, to explain to others the development of satipaṭṭhāna in daily life.

The householder Anāthapiṇḍika [5] is an example of someone who was intent not only on the welfare of himself, but also on the welfare of others. He was a very rich merchant of Sāvatthī who had presented the Jeta Grove to the Buddha. He developed satipaṭṭhāna in his daily life and became a sotāpanna. We read in the "Gradual Sayings" (V, Book of the Tens, Ch X, § 3, View) that he preached Dhamma to Wandering ascetics who held other views. They spoke to him about their own views, about the world being eternal, not eternal, limited, not limited, views about the soul and the body, and other speculative views. We read that Anāthapiṇḍika answered:

> "Sirs, when this or that worthy says: 'I hold this view, housefather: Eternal is the world'- such view arises either from his own lack of close thinking, or it depends on the words of someone else. A view like this has become, is put together, thought out, has arisen dependent on something. Now whatever has become, is put together, thought out, has arisen dependent on something- that is impermanent. What is impermanent, that is dukkha. To what is dukkha that worthy clings; to what is dukkha that worthy resorts...."

Anāthapiṇḍika said the same about the other views. Thereupon the wanderers asked him to tell them about his own view. He answered:

> "Sirs, whatsoever has become, is put together, is thought out, is dependent on something else, that is impermanent. What is impermanent, that is dukkha. What is dukkha, that is not of me, I am not that, not for me is that the self. Such is my own view, sirs."

[5] See for his story the Vinaya, V, Cullavagga, 6, on Lodgings, from 154.

> "Well, housefather, since you hold that whatsoever has become, put together... is impermanent, and since you hold that the impermanent is dukkha, then, housefather, you cling to dukkha, you make dukkha your resort."
>
> "Sirs, since whatsoever has become, whatsoever is put together, thought out, dependent on something else, is impermanent; since what is impermanent is dukkha; since what is dukkha is not of me, I am not that, not for me is that the self- thus is this matter well seen by me as it really is by right insight; and from that dukkha I have come to know the uttermost escape, as it really is."
>
> At these words the Wanderers kept silent, were confounded, hung the head, looked downward, were disappointed, sat unable to make reply.

Anāthapiṇḍika related his conversation with the wanderers to the Buddha and then the Buddha praised him. Afterwards the Buddha told the monks:

> "Monks, any monk who had been fully ordained in this dhamma-discipline even for a hundred rain-seasons might reasonably from time to time confute and rebuke the Wanderers holding other views just as they have been confuted by the housefather Anāthapiṇḍika."

When someone clings to speculative views it is only thinking, a nāma which is conditioned, impermanent, dukkha and non-self. When the wanderers tried to confuse Anāthapiṇḍika, telling him that he was clinging to what was dukkha, Anāthapiṇḍika explained that he did not take anything for self. Since he was a sotāpanna he understood the four noble Truths: dukkha, the origin of dukkha, the ceasing of dukkha and the way leading to the ceasing of dukkha. Thus he could say that he had come to know "the uttermost escape, as it really is".

It is most beneficial to listen to anyone who can explain the Dhamma in the right way, be he monk or lay-follower. Dhamma is Dhamma, it is the truth of realities as explained by the Buddha. We should not cling to a particular person who explains the Dhamma, it is the Dhamma itself which is important.

People of all ranks and classes, even slaves who had to do a great deal of menial work, could develop satipaṭṭhāna in daily life. We read in the "Stories of the Mansions" (Vimānavatthu, Khuddaka Nikāya, Minor Anthologies IV, Ch II, 1, Slave-woman's Mansion, Dāsīvimāna) about a slave-woman who developed insight and became a sotāpanna. We read in the "Commentary on the Vimāna Stories" (Paramatthadīpanī nāma Vimānavatthu-aṭṭhakatha, commentary on Ch II, 1, Exposition of the Servant-girl Vimāna) that, when the Buddha was dwelling at the Jeta Grove, a householder who lived at Sāvatthi listened to the Buddha and decided to give four constant supplies of food to the Order. He told his servant to be constantly diligent in this matter. We read:

> She was by nature endowed with faith, desirous of merit and virtuous; therefore day in, day out, she would rise very early, prepare the choicest food and drink, thoroughly sweep the monks' sitting-places, daub the floor-covering (of cow-dung), prepare the seats and, when the monks had arrived, would have them be seated there, salute them, worship them with scents, flowers, incense and lamps and then wait upon them with due care. Then one day when the monks had finished their meal she approached them, saluted them and then spoke thus, "Indeed how, sirs, is there complete release from the miseries of birth and so on?" Some monks gave her the Refuges and the Five Precepts and, making visible to her the true nature of the body, incited her as to recognition of its loathsomeness; others talked Dhamma-talk connected with impermanence. Keeping the precepts for sixteen years and properly striving time and again she one day gained the benefit of hearing Dhamma, developed vipassanā through the ripening of knowledge and realised the sotāpatti-fruit (fruition-consciousness of the sotāpanna).
>
> She died not long afterwards and came into being as a

> favourite attendant of Sakka, Lord of Devas....

We read in the Story of the Slave-woman's Mansion that Moggallāna saw the slave-woman as a deva, enjoying great bliss, and asked her the cause of her great beauty and the bliss she enjoyed. She answered:

> When I was born a human being among men, a woman slave I was, a menial in a household, a lay-follower of the One with Vision, of Gotama widely famed.
>
> With effort gained was I in the Dispensation of that steadfast one. Let this body break up as it may, herein is no relaxing (of effort).
>
> The Way of the five rules of training, secure, auspicious, is said by the wise to be without a thorn, without a tangle, straight.
>
> Behold the fruit of effort as achieved by a little woman. Companion of the king am I, of Sakka who is of the highhest power....

This slave-girl who had to do menial work gave us an example that for vipassanā we do not have to do anything special, that it is developed by being mindful of nāma and rūpa, no matter where and when. During the time someone is doing household chores there is the experience of tactile object through touch many times. At such moments there may be ignorance and forgetfulness, but sometimes there may be sati and paññā when there are conditions for their arising. The right conditions are listening to the Dhamma and right consideration of the Dhamma. When we touch something we may believe that it was there already for a long time, but from the Dhamma we learn that what is experienced through the bodysense is a rūpa which has arisen because of conditions and then falls away immediately. Hardness appears through the bodysense, but it falls away immediately. When it appears there can be mindfulness of it without thinking about it, and it can be understood as only a rūpa. When we think of this or that particular thing, such as a table, which is hard, it is a nāma which thinks, and it is due to the cetasika saññā, remembrance, that we recognize things and know how to use them. Hardness is an absolute reality, it has its own characteristic. Thinking and remembrance are absolute realities, they have their own characteristics. We do not have to name them when they appear; if there is direct awareness of them right understanding of their characteristics can gradually develop. The slave-girl we read about in the above-quoted sutta was not indolent but developed vipassanā with great patience and perseverance for many years. She was aware of realities over and over again so that the subsequent stages of vipassanā could arise and enlightenment be attained. We may have theoretical understanding of the fact that seeing is nāma and visible object is rūpa, that hearing is nāma and sound is rūpa, but it is necessary to develop right understanding of them when they appear at the present moment. When we stand, walk, take hold of a glass or saucepan, realities appear already, we do not have to go to a quiet place in order to be aware of nāma and rūpa.

We read in the "Middle Length Sayings" (III, no. 131, Discourse on the Auspicious) that the Buddha, while he was dwelling near Sāvatthī in the Jeta Grove, said to the monks:

> The past [6] should not be followed after, the future not desired.
>
> What is past is got rid of and the future has not come.
>
> But whoever has vision [7] now here, now there, of a present dhamma,
>
> Knowing that it is immovable, unshakable, let him cultivate it [8].
>
> Swelter at the task this very day. Who knows whether he will die tomorrow?
>
> There is no bargaining with the great hosts of Death.

[6] The commentary, the Papañcasūdanī, explains: the khandhas of the past.

[7] vipassati, that is, discerns with insight.

[8] In the translation of this sutta, in the "Wheel" no. 188, B.P.S. Sri Lanka, with the title "Ideal Solitude", "immovable" has been explained as the stable nature of the emancipated mind. The translation has here: The Immovable- the non-irritable. In that state should the wise one grow.

> Thus abiding ardently, unwearied day and night,
>
> He indeed is "Auspicious" called, described as a sage at peace.
>
> And how, monks, does one not follow after the past? He thinks: "Such was my rūpa ... my feeling... my perception (saññā)... my habitual tendencies (saṅkhārakkhandha)... my consciousness in the distant past" and finds delight therein. Even so, monks, does one follow after the past.
>
> The Buddha said that, if one does not find delight in the khandhas of the past, one does not follow after the past. Further on we read:
>
> And how, monks, does one desire the future? He thinks: "May my rūpa... feeling... perception... habitual tendencies... consciousness be thus in the distant future" and finds delight therein. Even so, monks, does one desire the future.

We then read that he who does not cling to khandhas of the future does not desire the future. Further on we read:

> And how, monks, is one drawn into present dhammas [9]? As to this, monks, an uninstructed ordinary person, taking no count of the pure ones, unskilled in the dhamma of the pure ones... regards rūpa... feeling... perception... the habitual tendencies... consciousness as self or self as having consciousness or consciousness as in self or self as in consciousness. Even so, monks, is one drawn into present dhammas.
>
> And how, monks, is one not drawn into present dhammas? As to this, monks, an instructed disciple of the pure ones, taking count of the pure ones, skilled in the dhamma of the pure ones, trained in the dhamma of the pure ones,

[9] The P.T.S. translation has: "drawn away among present things", but I prefer the Wheel translation: "drawn into present things". However, instead of "things" I retained the Pāli: dhammas.

> taking count of the true men, skilled in the dhamma of the true men, trained in the dhamma of the true men, does not regard rūpa... feeling... perception... the habitual tendencies... consciousness as self or self as having consciousness or consciousness as in self or self as in consciousness. Even so, monks, is one not drawn into present dhammas....

Taking the five khandhas for self is "personality belief" (sakkāya diṭṭhi)[10]. The sotāpanna has eradicated personality belief, and the only way leading to its eradication is mindfulness and right understanding of the dhamma appearing at the present moment. What is the dhamma appearing at the present moment? We read in "Mahākaccāna's Discourse on the Auspicious" (Middle Length Sayings III, no. 133) that, after the Buddha spoke the verse, "The past should not be followed after, the future not desired..." to the monk Samiddhi, Kaccāna the Great explained the meaning in detail, by way of the twelve sense-fields, āyatanas [11], namely: the five senses and the mind, and the objects experienced through the six doors. One may cling to the sense-fields of the past, of the future and of the present. He explained how one is not drawn into present dhammas:

> ...If, your reverences, there are at this present time both eyesense and visibile object... ear and sounds... nose and smells... tongue and flavours... body and tactile objects... mind and mental objects to which his consciousness is not bound fast by desire and attachment at this same present time, (then) because his consciousness is not bound fast by desire and attachment, he does not delight in them; not delighting in them, he is not drawn away among present dhammas. It is thus, your reverences, that one is not drawn into present dhammas.

Because of our accumulated ignorance we confuse visible object and seeing, sound and hearing, we cannot clearly distinguish their different

[10]See Ch 3.

[11]See Ch 2.Chapter 6

characteristics when they appear. So long as we do not distinguish nāma and rūpa from each other we will not be able to realize their arising and falling away. Then we will continue to cling to the idea of beings or things which last. When there can be awareness of one reality at a time appearing through one doorway we will begin to understand the present moment.

Chapter 6

The Four Applications of Mindfulness

We read in the "Kindred Sayings" (V, Mahā-vagga, Book III, Kindred Sayings on the Applications of Mindfulness, Ch I, § 1 Ambapālī) that the Buddha, while he was staying at Vesālī, in Ambapālī's Grove, said to the monks:

> This, monks, is the sole way that leads to the purification of beings, to the utter passing beyond sorrow and grief, to the destruction of woe and lamentation, to the winning of the Method, to realizing Nibbāna, to wit: the four applications of mindfulness. What four? Herein, a monk dwells, as regards body (as transient), having overcome, in the world, covetousness and grief. He dwells, as regards feelings... as regards cittas... as regards dhammas, contemplating dhammas (as transient), ardent, composed and mindful, having overcome, in the world, covetousness and grief. This, monks, is the sole way that leads to the purification of beings, to the utter passing beyond sorrow and grief, to the destruction of woe and lamentation, to the winning of the Method, to realizing Nibbāna, to wit: the four applications of mindfulness.

The four Applications of Mindfulness are: Mindfulness of Body, including all rūpas, Mindfulness of Feeling, Mindfulness of Citta and

Mindfulness of Dhammas. "Dhammas" include here all realities which are not classified under the first three Applications of Mindfulness; they are realities classified under different aspects, such as the akusala cetasikas which are the five "hindrances", the sobhana cetasikas which are the factors of enlightenment, the realities which are classified as the five khandhas or as the āyatanas, "sense-fields", or the four noble Truths . Thus, the four Applications of Mindfulness contain all realities which appear through the six doors of the senses and the mind and which can be objects of mindfulness. Whatever reality appears at the present moment can be object of mindfulness and right understanding. The development of right understanding of realities, satipaṭṭhāna, is the essence of the Buddha's teaching. The four Applications of Mindfulness have been explained in detail in the "Satipaṭṭhāna sutta"(Middle Length Sayings I, no 10) and the "Mahāsatipaṭṭhāna sutta"(Dialogues of the Buddha II, no. 22), but also many other parts of the scriptures contain expositions of the teaching of satipaṭṭhāna. Moreover, even when satipaṭṭhāna is not explicitly mentioned, it is implied, because it is the only way leading to the eradication of defilements, which is the goal of the Buddha's teachings. When one reads about the monk who "dwells contemplating" body, feelings, cittas and dhammas, one may think that one has to sit and meditate about the objects of satipaṭṭhāna. We read in the "Book of Analysis" (Ch 7, Analysis of the Foundation of Mindfulness, 195) a word exposition of "contemplating" and "dwells":

> "Contemplating" means: Therein what is contemplation? That which is wisdom, understanding, absence of dullness, truth investigation, right view. This is called contemplation. Of this contemplation he is possessed, well possessed, attained, well attained, endowed, well endowed, furnished. Therefore this is called "contemplating". "Dwells" means: Assumes the four postures, exists, protects, keeps going, maintains, turns about, dwells. Therefore this is called "dwells".

As we see, "dwells" does not refer only to sitting, but to the four postures, namely, walking, sitting, standing and lying down. In daily life these four postures are assumed time and again. Thus, he "dwells contemplating" means: it is his habit to be aware in his daily life of the realities included in the "Four Applications of Mindfulness". We read in the above quoted sutta: "having overcome in the world covetousness and grief". The "Book of Analysis", in the same section, explains the meaning of the "world":

> This same body is the world, also the five khandhas (as objects) of the attachments are the world.

The "world" includes all conditioned realities, nāmas and rūpas, which appear through the six doors. At the moment of mindfulness one is not attached to objects, there is no covetousness, nor is there grief or aversion. When there is mindfulness of whatever object presents itself, be it pleasant or unpleasant, there is no wish to flee from it or to go to a quiet place. However, some people feel that they are overwhelmed by defilements, especially when they are occupied with their daily tasks. They believe that they should calm the mind first before they develop vipassanā. They wonder whether they should not apply the Buddha's advice to dwell at the roots of a tree. It is true that we read for example in the "Middle Length Sayings" (I, no. 8, Discourse on Expunging) that the Buddha, while he was staying near Savatthi, in the Jeta Grove, taught Dhamma to Cunda and after that said:

> ...These, Cunda, are the roots of trees, these are empty places. Meditate, Cunda; do not be slothful; be not remorseful later. This is our instruction to you.

The Buddha spoke such words to monks. The monk should not be attached to the company of people, he should live like an arahat. The Buddha did not tell all monks to live in the forest because forest life is not suitable for everyone; one has to endure hardship and discomfort. Those who had accumulations for living in the forest and for developing samatha, tranquil meditation, could do so, but the Buddha did not lay down any rule as to mental development. Some people had accumulated the skill and inclination to develop both samatha and vipassanā, whereas others developed only vipassanā. In the same sutta the Buddha explained to Cunda about the attainment of jhāna, the result of the development of samatha:

> The situation occurs, Cunda, when a monk here, aloof from pleasures of the senses, aloof from unskilled states of mind, may enter on and abide in the first jhāna which is accompanied by initial thought and discursive thought , is born of aloofness, and is rapturous and joyful. It may occur to him: "I fare along by expunging." But these, Cunda, are not called expungings in the discipline for an ariyan; these are called "abidings in ease here-now" in the discipline for an ariyan.

The attainment of jhāna brings only temporary freedom from defilements, not the eradication of them. The Buddha spoke in a similar way about the higher stages of jhāna. After that the Buddha explained about restraint from all kinds of vices and defilements, about the development of wholesome qualities and the development of the eightfold Path. He taught the "disquisition on expunging...the disquisition on utter quenching". Through samatha defilements can be temporarily subdued, wheras through insight they can eventually be completely eradicated. There are many misunderstandings about the development of samatha. People want to have a peaceful mind, but they do not realize that this is attachment. They do not want to have aversion and worry, but they are ignorant of the disadvantages of attachment. It is attachment which conditions aversion. Even jhāna can be an object of clinging. We read in the "Middle Length Sayings" (III, 113, Discourse on the Good Man) that the Buddha, while he was staying near Sāvatthī, in the Jeta Grove, spoke to the monks about dhamma of good men and dhamma of bad men. The "bad man" is proud of the fact that he is of a high family, of his fame, of the monk's requisites he obtains. He exalts himself and disparages others because of these things, whereas the good man thinks of the goal of dhamma, does not exalt himself and does not disparage others. The bad man is proud of having heard much (of the teachings), of being an expert in Vinaya, a speaker on dhamma, a forest dweller, and he is proud of having attained jhāna. We read:

> And again, monks, a bad man, aloof from pleasures of the senses, aloof from unskilled states of mind, enters on and abides in the first jhāna which is accompanied by initial thought and discursive thought, is born of aloofness, and is rapturous and joyful. He reflects thus: "I am an acquirer of the attainment of the first jhāna, but these other monks are not acquirers of the attainment of the first jhāna." He exalts himself for that attainment of the first jhāna, disparages the others. This too, monks, is dhamma of a bad man. But a good man, monks, reflects thus: "Lack of desire even for the attainment of the first jhāna has been spoken of by the Lord; for whatever they imagine it to be, it is otherwise." He, having made lack of desire itself the main thing, neither exalts himself on account of that attainment of the first jhāna nor disparages others. This, too, monks, is dhamma of a good man...

The same is stated about the higher stages of jhāna. The bad man who attains the highest stage of immaterial jhāna, the plane of neither-perception-nor-non-perception exalts himself and disparages others. He cannot attain arahatship. The good man who attains the highest stage of immaterial jhāna is intent on detachment, he is not proud of his attainment. We read further on that the Buddha said:

> And again, monks, a good man, by passing quite beyond the plane of neither-perception-nor-non-perception, enters on and abides in the stopping of perception and feeling ; and when he has seen by means of wisdom his cankers are caused to be destroyed. And, monks, this monk does not imagine he is aught or anywhere or in anything....

This monk, who is a good man, will not be reborn, he has reached the end of the cycle of birth and death. When someone has accumulated the skill and the inclination to develop samatha to the degree of jhāna, he should not take jhānacitta for self and he should have no desire for jhāna. When jhānacitta arises it does so dependant on the appropriate conditions. He can be mindful of it in order to see it as it is, as non-self. For the development of jhāna many conditions have to be fulfilled and one should know which are impediments to jhāna. We read in the "Gradual Sayings" (V, Book of the Tens, Ch VIII, § 2, The thorn) that the Buddha was staying near Vesalī in Great Grove, at the House with the Peaked Roof, together with a number of senior monks. A crowd of Licchavis who were riding in their cars made a great noise, dashing into Great Wood to visit the Lord. The monks who were staying with the Buddha remembered that the Buddha had said that noise is an obstacle to jhāna, and therefore they retreated to Gosinga Wood where they would be free from noise and crowds. The Buddha asked the other monks where those senior monks were gone and then they gave him the reason for their departure. The Buddha said to them:

> Well said! Well said, monks! Those who should assert what those great disciples have asserted would rightly do so. Indeed, monks, I have said that noise is a thorn to jhāna . There are these ten thorns. What ten? To one who delights in seclusion delight in society is a thorn. To one devoted to concentration on the mark of the foul , concentration on the fair is a thorn. To one guarding the doors of the sense-faculties the sight of shows is a thorn. To the Brahma-life consorting with women is a thorn. To the first jhāna sound is a thorn; to the second jhāna applied thought and sustained thought ; to the third zest ; to the fourth jhāna in-breathing and out-breathing is a thorn. To the attainment of the stopping of perception and feeling, perception and feeling are a thorn. Lust, malice and delusion are thorns. So, monks, do you abide thornless, do you abide thorn-removers, do you abide thornless thorn-removers. Monks, the thornless are arahats, the thornless thorn-removers are arahats.

In this sutta the Buddha speaks about conditions for different stages of jhāna, and after that he reminds the monks that attachment, aversion and ignorance are hindrances. He reminds them to become people without defilements, namely arahats. The way leading to the eradication of defilements is satipaṭṭhāna. We read in the sutta that sound is a "thorn" to jhāna. Sound is not an obstacle to the development of insight. Someone may find a loud noise distracting from awareness of nāma and rūpa, but he forgets that sound can be object of awareness. He did not choose to hear such a sound, it just arose because of the appropriate conditions and it was the right time for kamma to produce the vipākacitta which heard that sound. We never know what object will present itself at a particular moment, realities do not belong to a self, they are beyond control. When we hear a loud noise aversion may arise, and that is another reality which arises because of conditions; there can be awareness of its characteristic so that it can be realized as non-self. We would like to ignore akusala, but we should face it with mindfulness and right understanding. If we are not mindful of akusala we will continue to take it for self and it will never be eradicated. We read in the "Mahā-satipaṭṭhāna sutta" (Dialogues of the Buddha, XXII) in the section on the fourth Application of Mindfulness, Mindfulness of Dhammas, that the monk has to see dhammas in dhammas. We read that he has to see "dhammas in dhammas from the point of view of the five hindrances". These are the defilements of sensuous desire, ill-will or anger, sloth and torpor, agitation and worry, and doubt. He has to realize it when there is sensuous desire in him and when he has no sensuous desire, and it is the same with the other hindrances. We read:

> ...So does he, as to dhammas, continue to consider them, both internally or externally, or internally and externally together. He ever considers how a dhamma is something that comes to be, again he ever considers how a dhamma is something that passes away, or he ever considers their coming to be with their passing away....

Whenever defilements arise they should be seen as dhammas, conditioned realities. We read in the above-quoted sutta that a monk should consider the origination and passing away of dhammas, he should see the impermanence of conditioned dhammas. What falls away immediately cannot be owned by a self. We can understand this truth on a theoretical level, but when there is direct awareness of the dhamma which appears the truth can be understood more deeply. When defilements are realized as dhammas which are impermanent and non-self, one will not be disturbed by them; one can face them with right understanding. Further on in the above-quoted sutta we read that a monk considers dhammas from the point of view of the five khandhas, of the "Six Internal and External Spheres of Sense" (āyatanas), of the Seven Factors of Enlightenment and of the four noble Truths. Under the section of the second noble Truth, the Truth of the origin of dukkha, which is craving, we read about all the objects of craving. The text states:

> And what, monks, is the ariyan Truth concerning the coming to be of dukkha? Even this craving, potent for rebirth, that is accompanied by lust and self-indulgence, seeking satisfaction now here, now there, namely, the craving for the life of sense, the craving for becoming (renewed life), and the craving for not becoming (for no rebirth). Now this craving, monks, where does it arise, where does it have its dwelling? In those material things of this world which are dear to us, which are pleasant. There does craving arise, there does it dwell. What things in this world are dear, what things are pleasant? The eye, the ear, the nose, the tongue, the body and the mind-these are the things in this world that are dear, that are pleasant. There does craving arise, there does it dwell. Visible object, sound, odour, flavour, tangible object and mind-object-these are the things in this world that are dear, that are pleasant. There does craving arise, there does it dwell. Seeing-consciousness, hearing-consciousness, smelling-consciousness, tasting-consciousness, body-consciousness and mind-consciousness, these are the things in this world that are dear, that are pleasant. There does craving arise, there does it dwell. Eye-contact, ear-contact, nose-contact, tongue-contact, body-contact and mind-contact- these are the things in this world that are dear, that are pleasant. There does craving arise, there does it dwell. Feel-

> ing originating from eye-contact, feeling originating from ear-contact, feeling originating from nose-contact, feeling originating from tongue-contact, feeling originating from body-contact, and feeling originating from mind-contact, these are the things in this world that are dear, that are pleasant. There does craving arise, there does it dwell. The remembrance of visible object, of sound, of odour, of flavour, of tangible object and of mental object-these are the things in this world that are dear, that are pleasant. There does craving arise, there does it dwell.

The same is said about intention (cetanā) concerned with the objects experienced through the six doors, craving for them, thinking about them, deliberating about them. We cling to the world appearing through the six doors. Every kind of craving can be considered as dhamma, it is included in the fourth Application of Mindfulness. We cannot force ourselves to be detached from pleasant objects, clinging is a conditioned reality. Clinging arises and falls away, but if there is no sati we do not know that it is a conditioned reality which is impermanent and non-self. We may understand in theory that it makes no sense to cling since pleasant objects only last for a very short while, but we still cling to all objects. Even when insight has been developed to the degree that paññā realizes the arising and falling away of realities, clinging is not eradicated yet. The sotāpanna sees realities as impermanent and non-self, he has eradicated the wrong view of self; but he still has craving for pleasant objects, and therefore he has to continue to develop insight until arahatship is attained. Only then all forms of clinging are eradicated. All the different sections of the "Mahā-satipaṭṭhāna sutta" remind us that whatever reality presents itself can be object of awareness and right understanding. Right understanding can be developed in any situation, no matter whether someone is developing calm or whether he is enjoying pleasant things such as music or delicious food. We read in the "Mahā-satipaṭṭhāna sutta" in the section on the Application of Mindfulness of the Body about the Reflection on the Repulsiveness of the Body:

> And moreover, monks, a monk reflects upon this very body,

> from the soles of his feet below upward to the crown of his head, as something enclosed in skin and full of various impurities:- "Here is in this body hair and down, nails, teeth, skin, flesh, sinews, bones, marrow, kidney, heart, liver, membranes, spleen, lungs, stomach, bowels, intestines; excrement, bile, phlegm, pus, blood, sweat, fat, tears, serum, saliva, mucus, synovic fluid, urine."...

The repulsiveness of the parts of the body is a meditation subject of samatha which has as its aim to be less attached to the body. However, when we notice "parts of the body", such as hair or nails, we can be reminded to develop insight in order to realize that what we take for "my body" are only elements which are impermanent and devoid of self. We read in the "Book of Analysis" (Ch 3, Analysis of the Elements, 82) about the element of solidity or hardness, here translated as "extension":

> Therein, what is the element of extension? The element of extension is twofold: It is internal; it is external. Therein what is internal element of extension? That which is personal, self-referable, hard, harsh, hardness, being hard, internal, grasped (by craving and false view). For example: head hair, body hair, nails, teeth, skin; flesh, sinews, bone, bone-marrow, kidneys; heart, liver, membraneous tissue, spleen, lungs; intestines, mesentery, undigested food, excrement; or whatever else there is, personal, self-referable, hard, harsh, hardness, being hard, internal, grasped. This is called internal element of extension...

It is then explained that the external element of extension is for example metal, stone or rock. The four Great Elements of solidity, cohesion, heat and motion are present in the body and also in material phenomena outside. Hardness of the body is the same as hardness of a rock, hardness is a paramattha dhamma, a rūpa with its own unchangeable characteristic. When hardness appears there can be awareness and right understanding of it as an element which is not "mine" or "self". In the "Mahā-satipaṭṭhāna sutta", after the section on the "Parts of the Body", it is said that the monk should dwell contemplating the arising and falling away of dhammas, and this is repeated after each section of the Applications of Mindfulness. Hair, nails and teeth are concepts we can think of, but they consists of rūpas which each have their own characteristic. Rūpa, the reality which does not know anything, is different from nāma, the reality which experiences something. The characteristics of nāma and rūpa have to be clearly distinguished from each other, not by theoretical understanding, but by insight, direct understanding, which has to be developed through awareness time and again. If nāma and rūpa are not clearly distinguished from each other, their arising and falling away, their impermanence, cannot be realized and we will continue to cling to the wrong view of self. Some people believe that the teaching of the four Applications of Mindfulness implies a particular order of objects of mindfulness; they believe that when someone is mindful of the objects included in Mindfulness of the Body, he is only aware of rūpa, not of nāma. However, there is no particular order of objects of mindfulness, it all depends on conditions which object presents itself at a particular moment. If there would be awareness of rūpa, but not of nāma, one would not really understand the characteristic of rūpa as completely different from the characteristic of nāma. Time and again, we notice parts of the body and also at such moments there are nāmas and rūpas which can be objects of mindfulness. The Buddha taught the four Applications of Mindfulness in order to remind us to be aware of rūpa, of feelings, of cittas, of dhammas, which include all realities other than those mentioned under the first three sections. At one moment there may be mindfulness of hardness, and at another moment mindfulness of feeling, which may be pleasant, unpleasant or indifferent, or mindfulness of the citta which experiences hardness, or mindfulness of aversion or attachment. There is time and again a reality impinging on one of the six doors. If there is right understanding of the objects of mindfulness, we can learn to be aware of one reality at a time, either a nāma or a rūpa. In that way their different characteristics can gradually be understood. This is the only way leading to the complete eradication of wrong view and the other defilements.

Appendix A

A.1 The Scriptures and Commentaries

The word of the Buddha, the Dhamma and the Vinaya as taught by him, consists of nine divisions, which are *Sutta*, *Geyya*, *Veyyākaraṇa*, *Gāthā*, *Udāna*, *Itivuttaka*, *Jātaka*, *Abbhuta* and **Vedalla*.[1]

Sutta[2] includes all Discourses, such as the "Mangala sutta" ("Good Omen Discourse," Minor Readings, V), and also the *Vinaya Piṭaka* [3] and the Niddesa.

Geyya includes all suttas with verses (gāthā), such as the Sagāthā-vagga of the Saṃyutta Nikāya or "Kindred Sayings".

Veyyākaraṇa or *Exposition* includes the *Abhidhamma Piṭaka*, the suttas without verses and the words of the Buddha that are not included in the other eight divisions.

Gāthā or *Verses* include the Dhammapada, Theragāthā, Therīgāthā (Psalms of the Brothers and Sisters) and those parts of the Sutta-Nipāta not called Sutta and entirely in verse.

[1] See "The Expositor," Atthasālinī Introductory Discourse, 26. The teachings as compiled (not yet written) literature are thus enumerated in the scriptures as nine divisions, for example in the "Middle Length Sayings" I, no. 22.

[2] The Pāli term sutta means that which is heard. The word of the Buddha which has been heard.

[3] The three Piṭaka, or *Tipiṭaka*, are the three divisions of the teachings, namely: *the Vinaya,Suttanta* and *Abhidhamma*. When the teachings are classified as nine divisions, the Vinaya is in a section of the *Sutta*. The Atthasālinī mentions the Sutta-Vibhaṅga and Parivāra in the section on Sutta, which belong to the Vinaya.

Udāna or *Verses of Uplift* include eighty-two suttas connected with verses recited by the Buddha, inspired by knowledge and joy.

Itivuttaka or *As it was said* includes one hundred ten suttas [4] beginning with "Thus it was said by the Blessed One" (in Pāli: "Vuttaṃ h'etaṃ Bhagavatā").

Jātaka or *Birth Stories* include five hundred fifty stories of the past lives of the Buddha and his disciples, beginning with the "Apaṇṇaka Jātaka."

Abbhuta, or *Marvellous*, includes suttas connected with wonderful and marvellous things (dhammas with extraordinary qualities, which are amazing).

Vedalla includes suttas with questions and answers that have as result understanding and delight, such as the Cullavedallasutta.

The word of the Buddha consists of eighty-four thousand units of text. The Venerable Ānanda learnt eighty-two thousand units of text from the Exalted One, and two thousand units of text from the bhikkhus, mainly from the Venerable Sāriputta. Each theme is one unit of text. Thus, the sutta containing one theme is one unit of text. Where there are questions and answers, each question forms one unit of text and each answer forms one unit of text.

When the scriptures are classified as the *Tipiṭaka*, they are classified as threefold, namely: the *Vinaya*, the *Suttanta* and the *Abhidhamma*. The *Vinaya Piṭaka* or *Books of Discipline* consist of five Books, namely:

- Parivāra (Appendix)
- Mahāvibhaṅga
- Bhikkhunī-vibhaṅga[5]
- Mahāvagga
- Cullavagga (Accessory)

[4] In the "Atthasālinī" the counting is one hundred and twelve.

[5] The P.T.S. has edited and translated these two books as three parts, the "Suttavibhaṅga."

The commentary that explains the *Vinaya* is the *Samantapāsādika.*[6]

The *Suttanta Piṭaka*, or *Discourses*, consists of five "Nikāyas"[7], namely, *Dīgha Nikāya* or *Dialogues of the Buddha*[8], *Majjhima Nikāya* or *Middle Length Sayings*[9], *Saṃyutta Nikāya* or *Kindred Sayings*[10], *Aṅguttara Nikāya* or *Gradual Sayings*[11], *Khuddaka Nikāya* or *The Minor Collection*[12].

The *Dīgha Nikāya* is a collection of long dialogues (dīgha means long), consisting of thirty-four suttas. This collection is divided into three sections (in Pāli: vagga)[13]:

- Sīla-kkhandha-vagga (sīla means morality and khandha means group);
- Mahā-vagga (mahā means great);
- Pāṭika-vagga (called after the first sutta; Pāṭika is a proper name).

The commentary to this collection is the *Sumaṅgalavilāsinī.*

The *Majjhima Nikāya* is a collection of suttas of medium length (majjhima means middle), and it consists of a hundred and fifty-two suttas. It is divided into three parts, which are called in Pāli "paṇṇāsa," meaning fifty. The first two parts consist of fifty suttas each and the third part of the fifty-two suttas. They are called:

- Mūla-paṇṇāsa (mūla means root), consisting of five sections of ten suttas;
- Majjhima-paṇṇāsa, consisting of five sections of ten suttas;

[6]The Introduction to the Vinaya, the Bāhiranidāna, has been translated as 'The Inception of Discipline and the Vinaya Nidāna', P.T.S.

[7]Nikāya means "body" or collection.

[8]I am giving the English titles, as used in the translations of the P.T.S. *The Dialogues of the Buddha* have been edited in three volumes

[9]Edited in three volumes.

[10]Edited in five volumes.

[11]Edited in five volumes.

[12]This collection consisting of sixteen parts has been edited in different volumes, but not all of them have been translated into English.

[13]These sections are in the Pāli text but not in the English edition.

- Upari-paṇṇāsa (upari means above or later), consisting of five sections, of which four have ten suttas and the fifth has twelve suttas.

The commentary to this collection is the *Papañcasūdanī.*

The *Saṃyutta Nikāya* is a group of suttas (saṃyutta means joined, connected) divided into five main divisions, namely:

- Sagāthā-vagga (gāthā means verse, with verses), with eleven sections;
- Nidāna-vagga (nidāna means origin or cause), consisting of nine sections;
- Khandha-vagga (dealing with the five khandhas), consisting of thirteen sections;
- Saḷāyatana-vagga (saḷāyatana is the sixfold āyatana or sense spheres), consisting of ten sections;
- Mahā-vagga (great chapter), consisting of twelve sections.

The commentary to this collection is the *Sāratthappakāsinī.*

The *Aṅguttara Nikāya* consists of suttas grouped according to the numbers of Dhamma subjects or points dealt with. They are arranged in order, from one to eleven. Thus, there are eleven "nipāta," or sections in all. "Book of the Ones" consists of suttas dealing with one kind of subject, and so on up to the Book of the Elevens. Summarizing them, they are:

- Eka-nipāta (eka means one), Book of the Ones;
- Duka-nipāta (duka, from dve, two, meaning pair), Book of the Twos;
- Tika-nipāta, Book of the Threes;
- Catuka-nipāta, Book of the Fours;
- Pañcaka-nipāta, Book of the Fives;

- Chaka-nipāta, Book of the Sixes;
- Sattaka-nipāta, Book of the Sevens;
- Aṭṭhaka-nipāta, Book of the Eights;
- Navaka-nipāta, Book of the Nines;
- Dasaka-nipāta, Book of the Tens;
- Ekādasaka-nipāta, Book of the Elevens.

The commentary to the *Aṅguttara Nikāya* is the *Manorathapūranī.* Apart from these four Nikāyas, there is the *Khuddaka Nikāya*, which contains the word of the Buddha.

This consists of the following books:

- Khuddakapāṭha or "Minor Readings";[14]
- Dhammapada (pada means word or phrase);[15]
- Udāna or "Verses of Uplift.";
- Itivuttaka or "As it was said.";
- Suttanipāta or "The Group of Discourses.";
- Vimānavatthu or "Stories of the Mansions" (in Minor Anthologies IV);
- Petavatthu or "Stories of the Departed" (in Minor Anthologies IV);
- Theragāthā or "Psalms of the Brethren.";
- Therīgāthā or "Psalms of the Sisters.";
- Jātaka or "Stories of the Buddha's Former Births" (in three volumes by P.T.S.);

[14]Translated into English and edited by the P.T.S. in one volume together with the translation of its commentary "The Illustrator of Ultimate Meaning."

[15]There are several English translations of this text.

- Mahā-Niddesa (niddesa means descriptive exposition);
- Cūḷa-Niddesa (cūḷa or culla means small);[16]
- Paṭisambhidāmagga or "The Path of Discrimination.";
- Apadāna (life histories);[17]
- Buddhavaṃsa or "Chronicle of the Buddhas" (in Minor Anthologies III);
- Cariyāpiṭaka or "Basket of Conduct" (in Minor Anthologies III);

The commentaries to these collections of the Khuddaka Nikāya are the following:

- *Paramatthajotikā*, which is the commentary to the Khuddakapātha and the Suttanipāta[18]
- *Dhammapadaṭṭhakathā* or "Buddhist Legends" (in three volumes by the P.T.S.) which is the commentary to the Dhammapada.
- *Paramatthadīpanī*, which is the Commentary to the Udāna, the Itivuttaka, the Petavatthu, the Theragāthā, the Therīgāthā, the Cariyāpiṭaka and the Vimānavatthu[19].
- *Jātakatthavaṇṇanā*, which is the commentary to the Jātaka[20];
- *Saddhammapajjotika*, which is the commentary to the Mahā-Niddesa and the Cūḷa-Niddesa;

[16]The Mahā-Niddesa and the Cūḷa-Niddesa have not been translated into English.

[17]This has not been translated into English.

[18]The commentary to the Khuddakapātha has been translated into English as I mentioned. The commentary to the Sutta Nipāta has been translated by Ven. Bodhi.

[19]Translated into English are: the Udāna commentary (two volumes), the Itivuttaka commentary (two volumes), the commentary to the Vimānavatthu, "Vimāna Stories," the commentary to the Petavatthu, "Peta Stories," the commentary to the Therīgāthā, "Commentary on the Verses of the Therīs."

[20]In the English edition of the Buddha's Birth Stories, parts of the commentary have been added.

- *Saddhammappakāsinī*, which is the commentary to the Paṭisambhidāmagga;
- *Visuddhajanavilāsinī*, which is the commentary to the Apadāna;
- *Madhuratthavilāsinī*, or *The Clarifier of Sweet Meaning* (P.T.S.), which is the commentary to the Buddhavaṃsa.

Abhidhamma Piṭaka consists of the following seven Books:

- *Dhammasaṅgaṇī* (translated by PTS as *Buddhist Psychological Ethics*, and also translated by U Kyaw Khine) and this has as commentary the *Aṭṭhasālinī* (*Expositor*);
- *Vibhaṅga* or *The Book of Analysis*, which has as commentary the Sammohavinodanī or *Dispeller of Delusion*[21];
- *Dhātukathā* or *Discourse on Elements*;
- *Puggalapaññatti* or *a Designation of Human Types*;
- *Kathāvatthu* or *Points of Controversy*;
- *Yamaka* or *The Book of Pairs*; [22]
- *Paṭṭhāna* or *Conditional Relations*;[23]

As to the commentary to the last five Books of the Abhidhamma, this is the *Pañcappakaraṇatthakathā*[24]

The greater part of the commentaries to the Tipiṭaka is from the hand of the great commentator Buddhaghosa[25]. He translated into

[21] In two volumes.

[22] Yamaka means "Pair." This has been translated into English in Myanmar by U narada, Mūla Paṭṭhana and pupils. Also PTS is producing a translation of the Yamaka in three parts: The Book of Pairs and its Commentary: A translation of the Yamaka and Yamakappakaraṇaṭṭhakathā by C.M.M. Shaw & L.S. Cousins, 2018. Only the first part has been finished.

[23] There is a translation of part of the Paṭṭhāna. There is also a "Guide to Conditional Relations", explaining part of the Paṭṭhāna, by U Narada, Myanmar.

[24] Only the commentary to the Kathāvatthu has been translated into English, with the title of "Debates Commentary"

[25] He lived in the fifth century of the Christian era and stayed in the"Great Monastery" of Anurādhapura, in Sri Lanka.

Pāli, compiled and arranged material from the ancient commentaries, which were in Sinhalese. These commentaries, the Mahā-Atthakathā, the Mahā- Paccarī and the Kuruṇḍi, stemmed from the time of the Thera Mahinda, the son of the great King Asoka who came to Sri Lanka in order to propagate Buddhism.

Furthermore, there are sub-commentaries, called ṭīkā in Pāli, which explain the commentaries. These are the Sāratthadīpanī, a sub-commentary to the Samantapāsādikā, which is the commentary to the Vinaya, the Sārattha Mañjūsā, a sub-commentary to the Suttanta Piṭaka, the Paramatthapakāsinī, a sub-commentary to the Abhidhamma Piṭaka, and the anuṭīkā (anu meaning: along, alongside), which explains words and expressions in the subcommentaries. Apart from the aforementioned works there are several other texts in Buddhism needed for the study of the Dhamma that were composed by the "Elders"[26] who were qualified to pass on the tradition of the Dhamma. These are the following texts:

- *Milindapañha* or *Milinda's Questions*[27], composed about 500 Buddhist Era (43 B.C.);
- *Visuddhimagga* or *Path of Purification*[28], an Encyclopedia on Buddhism, composed by Buddhaghosa about 1000 B.E. (457 A.D.);
- *Abhidhammattha Saṅgaha* or *A Manual of Abhidhamma*[29], composed by Ven. Anuruddha about 1000 B.E. (457 A.D.)[30];

[26]Thera can be translated as Elder or senior monk, a monk who has been ordained for at least ten years.

[27]In two volumes. One translation by the P.T.S. and another one by T.W. Rhys Davids.

[28]One edition as translated by Ven. Nyāṇamoli, Colombo, and one edition as translated by Pe Maung Tin, P.T.S.

[29]It has been translated into English and published by the P.T.S. with the title of *Compendium of Philosophy*, and by Ven. Nārada, Colombo, under the title of *A Manual of Abhidhamma*. It has also been translated by the Venerable Bhikkhu Bodhi as *A Comprehensive Manual of Abhidhamma*. Moreover, it has been translated together with its commentary as *Summary of the Topics of Abhidhamma* and *Exposition of the Topics of Abhidhamma*, by R.P. Wijeratne and Rupert Gethin.

[30]The P.T.S. edition suggests that the date is between the 8th and the 12th century A.D.

- *Sārattha Saṅgaha*, composed by Ven. Nanda about 1000 B.E. (457 A.D.);
- *Paramattha Mañjūsā*, a sub-commentary to the *Visuddhimagga*, composed by the Ven. Dhammapāla.
- *Saccasaṇkhepa* (meaning Exposition of the Truth), composed by Ven. Dhammapāla [31];
- *Abhidhammattha-vibhāvinī-ṭīkā*, a sub-commentary to the Abhidhammattha Saṅgaha composed by Sumangala, of Sri Lanka;
- *Moha Vicchedanī*, an explanation of the Dhammasangaṇi and the Vibhaṅga (the first and second Books of the Abhidhamma), composed by Ven. Kassapa of Sri Lanka, about 1703 B.E. (1160 A.D.);
- *Mangalattha Dīpanī*, an explanation of the Mangala sutta (Good Omen Discourse, Khuddakapāṭha, Minor Readings, no 5) composed by Ven. Sirimangala in Chiangmai.

I could add to this enumeration the Nettippakaraṇa, translated as "The Guide," P.T.S. and the Peṭakopadesa which has been translated as "Piṭaka Disclosure" by Ven. Ñaṇamoli. They are compilations of a school, which, according to tradition, traced its descent to Mahā-Kaccana, one of the great disciples of the Buddha. Dhammapāla has written a commentary on the Netti, probably late fifth century A.D.

[31] Translated into English by by R.P. Wijeratne and Rupert Gethin, see footnote 29.

A.2 Books written by Nina van Gorkom

- *Buddhism in Daily Life* A general introduction to the main ideas of Theravada Buddhism.The purpose of this book is to help the reader gain insight into the Buddhist scriptures and the way in which the teachings can be used to benefit both ourselves and others in everyday life.

- *Abhidhamma in Daily Life* is an exposition of absolute realities in detail. Abhidhamma means higher doctrine and the book's purpose is to encourage the right application of Buddhism in order to eradicate wrong view and eventually all defilements.

- *Cetasikas* Cetasika means 'belonging to the mind'. It is a mental factor which accompanies consciousness (citta) and experiences an object. There are 52 cetasikas. This book gives an outline of each of these 52 cetasikas and shows the relationship they have with each other.

- *The Buddhist Teaching on Physical Phenomena* A general introduction to physical phenomena and the way they are related to each other and to mental phenomena. The purpose of this book is to show that the study of both mental phenomena and physical phenomena is indispensable for the development of the eightfold Path.

- *The Conditionality of Life* By Nina van Gorkom This book is an introduction to the seventh book of the Abhidhamma, that deals with the conditionality of life. It explains the deep underlying motives for all actions through body, speech and mind and shows that these are dependent on conditions and cannot be controlled by a 'self'. This book is suitable for those who have already made a study of the Buddha's teachings.

- *Letters on Vipassanā* A compilation of letters discussing the development of vipassanā, the understanding of the present moment, in daily life. Contains over 40 quotes from the original scriptures and commentaries.

A.3 Books translated by Nina van Gorkom

- *A Survey of Paramattha Dhammas* by Sujin Boriharnwanaket. A Survey of Paramattha Dhammas is a guide to the development of the Buddha's path of wisdom, covering all aspects of human life and human behaviour, good and bad. This study explains that right understanding is indispensable for mental development, the development of calm as well as the development of insight.

- *The Perfections Leading to Enlightenment* by Sujin Boriharnwanaket. The Perfections is a study of the ten good qualities: generosity, morality, renunciation, wisdom, energy, patience, truthfulness, determination, loving-kindness, and equanimity.

www.ingramcontent.com/pod-product-compliance
Lightning Source LLC
Chambersburg PA
CBHW032047040426
42449CB00007B/1019
* 9 7 8 1 8 9 7 6 3 3 3 5 9 *